OAKWOOD LIBRARY OF RAILWAY HIS

Isle of P
Railways

Volume One
The Admiralty
and
Quarry Railways

B.L. Jackson

THE OAKWOOD PRESS

British Library Cataloguing in Publication Data
A Record for this book is available from the British Library
ISBN 0 85361 540 3

Typeset by Oakwood Graphics.
Repro by Ford Graphics, Ringwood, Hants.
Printed by Cambrian Printers, Aberystwyth, Dyfed.

Removing the 'overburden' before quarrying can commence. Small tip waggons on 2 ft gauge track hauled by horses often undertook this type of work.   *Author's Collection*

Title page: The original stone blocks used to support the rails of the 'Merchants' Railway' on the upper level of the formation around the Verne, still in position in 1999.   *Author*

Front cover: A delightful colour postcard view of the bottom of the 'Merchants' Railway' incline c. 1900.   *Author's Collection*

Rear cover, top: Convicts at work in the Admiralty Quarries, Portland. *Author's Collection*

Rear cover, bottom: The original breakwaters viewed in 1989. In the foreground the remains of East Weare Batteries. Below several of the original buildings still survive in the dockyard. In the background, the Inner Breakwater, the South entrance, and the Outer Breakwater with its fort at the far end.   *Author*

Published by The Oakwood Press, P.O. Box 13, Usk, Mon., NP15 1YS.
E-mail: oakwood-press@dial.pipex.com
Website: http://ds.dial.pipex.com/oakwood-press

Contents

A scene from a bygone age, quarrymen stand by a loaded waggon. On the left is Robert Gibbs, in the centre stand his two sons Jack and Bob, to the right Jack Gibbs, brother of Robert Gibbs.   *Author's Collection*

Acknowledgements

To assemble a work of this nature reference has been made to a great many documents, books, newspapers and other sources. The Minute books of the Portland Railway Company, together with many documents at the Public Record Office have been consulted, as have the three principal local newspapers, the *Southern Times*, *Dorset County Chronicle*, and *Dorset Evening Echo*.

Previously published works include:

Railways of Dorset by J.H. Lucking (RCTS)
The Great Western at Weymouth by J.H. Lucking (David & Charles)
The *Royal Navy at Portland* by G. Carter (Maritime Books)
Various publications of the Industrial Railway Society
Various publications of the Industrial Locomotive Society
The Quarrying of Portland Stone by P. Trim
The Wotton Tramway by K. Jones
Burrell Showman's Road Locomotives by M.R. Lane
The Undertype Steam Wagon by M.A. Kelley
Various publications of The Road Locomotive Society.

The assistance of the following organisations is gratefully acknowledged:

Dorset County Council Archives Department
Dorset County Library Service
Dorset County Museum
Weymouth & Portland Museum services
Public Record Office (Kew)
HMS *Osprey*
Royal Engineers Library, Chatham.

The local studies department of Weymouth library has been of great assistance, in particular Mrs Maureen Attwooll, whose vast knowledge of local history is invaluable, as have many Portlanders, including Messrs Edward Andrews, Stuart Morris, and Peter Trim who are experts on the Island's history, and the late Mr Davis, former Secretary of the Portland Railway for allowing consultation of the company minute books.

Thanks are also due to George Pryer for his work on the diagrams and his expert assistance on railway matters, Michael Tattershall deserves special thanks for much hard work on the manuscript in the early stages. Messrs A. Civil, M. Cook, and F. Jones of the Industrial Locomotive Society have been of great assistance.

I am also grateful to the following for their assistance with the work, C.L. Caddy, T.H. Cailes, E.D.K. Coombe, George Davey, R. Diment, 'Skylark' Durston, Peter Legg, R.C. Link, K. Lynham, Bill Macey, M. Marshall, Col J.E. Nowers, B. Thirlwall, J. Thompson, R.C. Riley, P. Webb and Bob Wollage.

Finally I should like to thank my wife, herself a Portlander, for her encouragement and help whilst this work was being written.

Sadly as this work was being completed Peter Trim passed away following a long fight against indifferent health. A true Portlander, Peter's life revolved around the island community, its history and traditions. A long serving member of the Court Leet, he was also Chairman of the trustees of the Portland Heritage Trust, and an acknowledged expert in Island History. Therefore this work is dedicated to Peter Ronald Trim, 1945-1998.

Introduction

For such a compact place, the Isle of Portland contained a wide variety of early forms of heavy transport, and although this book is ostensibly a history of the 'Merchants' Railway', the railways to construct the breakwater and serve the Dockyard, and the other assorted narrow and standard gauge lines that served the quarries and other needs of the island, traction engines were inextricably involved with the movement of stone to the various railway loading points. They therefore form part of the story which would not be complete without reference to the famous stone trade and the Naval establishments. It is against this complex background that this history has been compiled, and although each system has been dealt with separately, it is inevitable that certain events are mentioned several times in the context of each system.

Added to the industrial lines was the main railway from Weymouth which will be dealt with in a separate volume. However to set the scene, the railway arrived at Portland (Victoria Square) in October 1865, a mixed gauge branch from Weymouth owned by the Weymouth & Portland Railway Company but operated jointly by the Great Western and London & South Western companies. An extension to Easton was first planned in 1867 by the inaccurately named Easton & Church Hope Railway Company; after a long financial struggle the line was completed to Easton for goods traffic in October 1900 and opened to passenger traffic two years later. Both companies retained their separate identities until 1948!

The author does not claim this work to be the Alpha and Omega, as much interesting information has disappeared with the passage of time. Indeed, being industrial railways, not all details were recorded as they were with main line concerns who were answerable to the Board of Trade and other authorities.

Research of this material has taken over 30 years, and the author has been very dependent on access to those documents that survive, supplemented by the memories of people concerned with the line. As the years go by the likelihood of new information coming to light becomes ever more slight, and the time has come to go to print with what is known.

It is hoped this book will meet the requirements of those who seek a general history of the industrial railways of the Isle of Portland, and also clearly illustrates the working conditions of the era and how industrial relations have changed since the 19th century.

B.L. Jackson
Weymouth
1999

Although the 'Merchants' Railway' has ceased to exist for many years, many of the wheels from the waggons have found a useful existence as sinkers used to hold boat moorings at both Weymouth and Portland.   *Author*

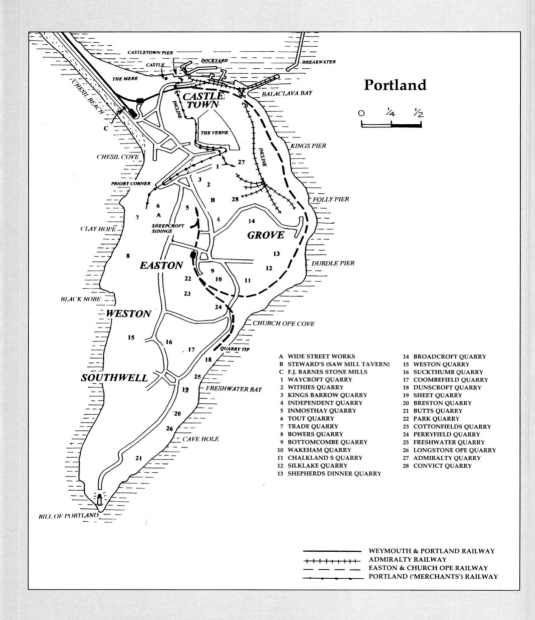

Portland

0   ¼   ½

CASTLETOWN PIER
CASTLE
DOCKYARD
BREAKWATER
THE MERE
BALACLAVA BAY
CHESIL BEACH
CASTLE TOWN
INCLINE
THE VERNE
KINGS PIER
C
CHESIL COVE
INCLINE
PRIORY CORNER
FOLLY PIER
CLAY HOPE
SHEEPCROFT SIDINGS
GROVE
EASTON
DURDLE PIER
BLACK NORE
WESTON
CHURCH OPE COVE
SOUTHWELL
QUARRY TIP
FRESHWATER BAY
CAVE HOLE
BILL OF PORTLAND

A WIDE STREET WORKS
B STEWARD'S (SAW MILL TAVERN)
C F.J. BARNES STONE MILLS
1 WAYCROFT QUARRY
2 WITHIES QUARRY
3 KINGS BARROW QUARRY
4 INDEPENDENT QUARRY
5 INMOSTHAY QUARRY
6 TOUT QUARRY
7 TRADE QUARRY
8 BOWERS QUARRY
9 BOTTOMCOMBE QUARRY
10 WAKEHAM QUARRY
11 CHALKLAND S QUARRY
12 SILKLAKE QUARRY
13 SHEPHERDS DINNER QUARRY

14 BROADCROFT QUARRY
15 WESTON QUARRY
16 SUCKTHUMB QUARRY
17 COOMBEFIELD QUARRY
18 DUNSCROFT QUARRY
19 SHEET QUARRY
20 BRESTON QUARRY
21 BUTTS QUARRY
22 PARK QUARRY
23 COTTONFIELDS QUARRY
24 PERRYFIELD QUARRY
25 FRESHWATER QUARRY
26 LONGSTONE OPE QUARRY
27 ADMIRALTY QUARRY
28 CONVICT QUARRY

———————— WEYMOUTH & PORTLAND RAILWAY
+++++++++ ADMIRALTY RAILWAY
– – – – – – EASTON & CHURCH OPE RAILWAY
–·–·–·–·– PORTLAND ('MERCHANTS') RAILWAY

Map showing the various quarries and other places of importance on the Island.

Chapter One

Portland and the Stone Industry

Portland is an island, a solid block of limestone four miles long and 1¾ miles wide covering 2,999 acres, projecting out into the English Channel south of Weymouth on the Dorset Coast. The North face reaches a height of 500 feet above sea level.

There is evidence that Portland was occupied during both the Bronze and Iron ages, and also during the Roman period, whilst Viking raids were not uncommon between 795 and 840 AD. However, the first documented details of the Island appear in Domesday Book, where it is recorded that the King held the Island as a single Royal Manor.

Although always referred to as an Island, it is in fact joined to the mainland by Chesil Bank - a massive ridge of pebbles stretching out to the west from Portland to West Bay, a distance of some 18 miles. Between the Chesil Bank and the mainland there is a narrow strip of water known as the 'Fleet', which ends at Abbotsbury where the pebble ridge meets land, and it is this that cuts Portland off from neighbouring Weymouth. Prior to the opening of a bridge (known as the Ferrybridge) in 1839, the only way to travel to Portland was by boat from Weymouth or by way of the ferry provided at Wyke Regis. Sometimes the latter crossing could be very difficult and dangerous, as the currents are very fast-flowing at the mouth of the Fleet.

The waters off Chesil Bank have always been dangerous, many ships being wrecked and hundreds of lives lost in the area, as the gravestones in the churchyards at Wyke Regis and Portland testify! For example, on the night of 18th November, 1795, Admiral Christian lost a fleet of ships on the beach which resulted in a great many persons being drowned. Disasters of this magnitude remained frequent even after steam replaced sail, and in January 1920 three steamships were swept ashore by the angry sea, two of which were a total loss. Many are the tales of smuggling and the looting of vessels stranded on the beach that have become part of the folklore of the Island, but it should be remembered that in times of distress and danger Portlanders have more often than not risked (and sometimes lost) their own lives in attempting to rescue people from the cruel sea.

One Colonel Christopher Lilley, who surveyed the Island in 1715, reported, 'It comprises of five little villages with one Parish Church, populated by about 750 people, who, in the main are employed in the quarries'. Until the late 1800s it was an insular society, and until transport improved few people ever left or visited the Island, people from the outside being called 'Kimberlins' by the Portlanders. Islanders very rarely married anyone from the mainland, and over the years this developed a very close inter-relationship of families.

The census of 1851 reveals that the most common family names on the Island were Attwooll, Comben, Pearce, Stone and White. The largest number of Stones (74) lived in Wakeham, Pearces (80) in Easton, and 94 Whites in Chiswell, whilst Combens were fairly evenly distributed - the majority living 'Underhill'. Of the 144 Attwoolls, 36 lived in Wakeham.

However in later years the influx of service personnel and prison officers' families, together with the greater mobility of families in general, quickly broadened the previously tight-knit community.

It was this isolation from the mainland that gave Portland its own individual way of life which lasted in many respects until the Great War. One unusual feature was the 'Court Leet', which is believed to be of Saxon origin, the main purpose of which was to control and manage the Common Land and collect the rights due to the Royal Manor. The Court consisted of a Foreman, a Reeve, a Chief Constable, and 24 jurymen, and it formed a sort of Island police force. The duties of the Court Leet have greatly diminished, and it has little power today due to the present system of local government, but it remains in being as a traditional body which meets once a year during November.

In the past the wrath of the Court Leet could be severe if a wrongful act was committed. For instance, it is recorded that in October 1826, one Elizabeth Pearce was fined 6s. 8d. for allowing her sheep to enter into the stubble fields before the 10th of that month, and similar fines were not uncommon. In times when landowners had to provide men and arms for war, Portland was exempted by paying 'Quit' rent, a sum of £4 14s. 3d. which was collected annually by the Reeve. This payment continued for many hundreds of years and was not extinguished until the 1920s, when the Islanders were told that for a lump sum their 'Quit' rent would be commuted for all time. The offer was taken up, and it was argued that Portlanders were exempt from National Service because of this payment, although there is no record of anyone refusing to serve in the forces on these grounds.

Isolation also created a great number of traditions, peculiar customs and beliefs, and allowed them to survive long after such things had died out in other parts of the Country. Witchcraft was prevalent well into the 19th century, for in 1856 fifty members of the Methodist Church were expelled by the Minister because of their beliefs, and the following year a 20-year-old youth was convicted at the County Quarter Sessions for acts of witchcraft.

When John Smeaton - the builder of the Eddystone Lighthouse - came to Portland to obtain stone he was amazed by the customs and beliefs of the inhabitants, but he also admired the health and strength of the quarrymen, and when he asked how they could pick up such a stout set of men, the guide replied,

> If you knew how these men were produced you would wonder less, for all our marriages are productive of children. Our people here are bred up to hard labour, and are very early in a condition to marry and provide for a family. They intermarry with one another, very rarely going to the mainland to seek a wife. It has been the custom of the Island from time immemorial that they never marry until fertility is proven.

It was the opening of the first bridge to replace the ferry in 1839, and the coming of the railway to the Island in 1865, that did so much to alter the local way of life. The Industrial Revolution had already wrought great changes across most of the Country, and it came to Portland very suddenly with the construction of the breakwater, the convict prison, the railway, and the use of steam power (which advanced the methods of quarrying), coupled with the

One of a series of comic postcards produced in 1919, taking a facetious look at life on the island. This one depicts the arrival of convicts. *Author's Collection*

influx of labour that came with this new technology. The railway also advanced the stone masonry trade, as it then became possible to transport finished work away from the island with a much reduced risk of damage.

The arrival of the ships of the Royal Navy which followed the construction of the breakwater caused great changes in the local way of life. The population increased rapidly, from 2,852 in 1841 to 8,468 twenty years later. By the turn of the century it had reached 15,199, of which 6,587 were either Naval, Military or prison personnel. The Royal Navy had transformed its ships into the finest steam powered fleet in the World, and instead of the breakwater forming a shelter for sailing ships, as it had done originally, it became a port where the mighty ships came to collect fuel. Portland had become a coaling station for the fleet.

Further changes took place in the 20th century. In 1921 the convict prison became a Borstal Institution, whilst the Verne Citadel - a concealed Army Barracks - was relinquished by the Army and converted into a civil prison after World War II. Eventually the vast fleet of ships that used to assemble at Portland started to decline, and the establishment that had developed over the years into a full-scale dockyard was reduced to a Naval Base. It finally closed during 1996, together with other Admiralty establishments.

The demand for stone also declined, although a new product called 'Portcrete' - a reinforced concrete - went some way towards replacing it as an Island industry, but many of the quarries have closed, a result of the ever changing world of the building trade. The closure of the Royal Naval Air station early in 1999 marked the end of a commitment by the armed forces to the island. The former Naval Base has been opened as a commercial port which has yet to develop.

Today the Island relies on the Prison Service for its main source of employment. Ironically, the Prison Service which first came here to assist in the construction of the harbour of refuge, is now 150 years later the principal employer. Following the closure of the Naval Base, a floating prison (the controversial 'prison ship') arrived to give the Island its third penal establishment. Local government reform has joined the 48,400 population of Weymouth with the 12,700 of Portland to form a combined Borough, and much has changed. Numerous cars and buses now take holidaymakers and day trippers from Weymouth to Portland during the summer months to look around the Island, that unusual place which Thomas Hardy once described as 'The Gibraltar of Wessex'.

The Stone Industry

As stone was the principal industry, and one of the main reasons for the construction of the island's railways, a brief description of its history and development is not out of place.

The basic constituents of Portland stone are 95.8 per cent Calcium Carbonate, 1.2 per cent Magnesium Carbonate, 1.2 per cent Silica. 0.3 per cent Aluminium and Iron Oxides, plus 1.4 per cent water and loss. To reach the best material, known as 'base' or 'whitebed', 12 layers of various types of soil and stone have to be removed. The use of Portland stone dates back to very early times. During the Roman period Portland stone was taken at least as far as Dorchester. It was also used in the building of Exeter Cathedral in the 14th century, for the building of the Royal Palace of Westminster in 1347, for London Bridge several years later, and Inigo Jones' Great Banqueting Hall at Whitehall in 1622.

During the early part of the 17th century Portland stone was used extensively for many private and public buildings in London and other large cities. At this period most of the stone was quarried from the east side of the Island, this being best suited for gaining access to the sea for shipment - an important consideration in view of the difficulties of internal transport. Between 1619 and 1622, £7,000 was spent on building a new pier to facilitate the loading of stone onto ships, all exports having to be taken by sea as no bridge to the mainland existed until 1839.

The Great Fire of London (1666) created a huge demand for Portland stone for the rebuilding of the City, especially in the reconstruction of St Paul's Cathedral by Sir Christopher Wren, and by 1700 no less than 50,332 tons of it had been used in this work. While the quarrying of the stone for St Paul's continued, several disputes with the Islanders arose over the levy paid for the material, it being claimed that the stone was for the King's own use. But the Islanders thought otherwise, and became so aggravated that in 1678 they sabotaged the waggons, piers and cranes.

In 1703 an attempt was made to stop all quarrying on Portland save with the consent of Sir Christopher Wren, it being feared that the quantity of good stone available would be insufficient to complete St Paul's unless strict control was exercised. This caused more trouble on the Island, and the quarrymen succeeded in getting the proposal withdrawn.

As the quality and quantity of stone from the east side of the Island gradually diminished the heart of the industry moved further into the centre of Portland, but the piers were still situated on the east side and consequently transportation became very difficult.

The Reverend J. Skinner, Rector of the village of Camerton in Somerset, visited Portland in 1804 and wrote of his observations.

Large hewn stones lie scattered in all directions, indeed the quarries worked on the Island are prodigious, and the mode of conveying the ponderous masses down the steep slopes unavoidably arrests the attention of the stranger: the blocks being placed on a strong wooden carriage, with solid wheels apportionate to the weight they are to sustain. Two horses are harnessed, one before and one (and sometimes two) behind, the latter being supplied with strong breeching in order to act as drawbacks to the carriage, and prevent its running with too great a velocity down the steep hills. Indeed, the sagacity and exertions of these poor animals in this arduous employment is really astonishing; they squat down on their haunches and suffer themselves to be dragged for many yards, struggling with all their strength against the weight that forces them forwards. To one unaccustomed to the sight, it appears as though their limbs must inevitably be dislocated, or their sinews cracked by the violence of their exertions: Indeed, one is compassionate to these poor creatures, the rather as all this labour might easily be obviated by the simple construction of a rail-road. Why this has not been long since performed is to me surprising, especially as Portland stone is in universal request.

Throughout the Victorian period the demand for Portland stone was to increase as towns and cities erected magnificent public and private buildings. In London, Tower Bridge, The Law Courts, the Public Record Office, the National Gallery and many other well known buildings were the products of Portland. Following World War I the Cenotaph in Whitehall and many other memorials and gravestones for the War Graves Commission were produced on the Island.

Again in the years between the wars vast amounts of stone were sent to construct some of the finest buildings around the world. In London Broadcasting House, The Tate Gallery, and the new frontages in Regent Street are a lasting reminder of the quarryman's skill. Following World War II stone to rebuild blitzed cities was required, and once more headstones for the War Graves Commission came from the island, as did stone for the Kennedy Memorial at Runnymede. Unfortunately, like other sections of the building and construction industry, it was subject to the economics of the time and so suffered its share of short time working, the laying-off of staff, and shut-downs. At the end of 1932 it was reported that over 1,500 men were wholly or partly unemployed. By the end of June 1933 nearly half the quarries were closed and many of the remainder only working half time. *The Dorset Daily Echo* for 17th June stated, '. . . seventy-four young quarrymen who have been wholly unemployed for over six months, have to face the means test on Monday'.

However, Portland stone is always in demand, albeit on a smaller scale, for certain building requirements and the maintenance of older structures.

Originally many of the quarries were small family-run affairs. It was recorded in 1840 that there were 56 quarries on the island employing 240 men, of which 138 worked for the Stewards - a family which could trace its history back to supplying stone for St Paul's Cathedral.

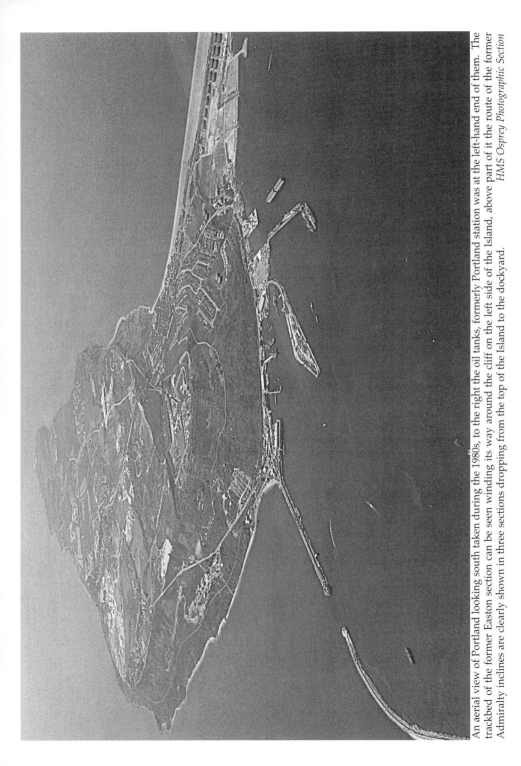

An aerial view of Portland looking south taken during the 1980s, to the right the oil tanks, formerly Portland station was at the left-hand end of them. The trackbed of the former Easton section can be seen winding its way around the cliff on the left side of the Island, above part of it the route of the former Admiralty inclines are clearly shown in three sections dropping from the top of the Island to the dockyard.   *HMS Osprey Photographic Section*

By the late 19th century the small firms were joining forces as trade developed. The Portland Stone Company, which had been formed during 1872, was taken over in 1885 by one of its employees, F.J. Barnes, who at the time was only 22 years of age! Barnes later acquired the Stone Working & Quarrying Company in 1891.

In 1890 Messrs Webber & Pangbourne, London stone merchants, established a sawmills and masonry yard at Park Road, Easton. At the same time on land nearby the John Pearce Stone Company opened a new masonry yard.

The formation in December 1887 of the Bath Stone Company, a combine of seven quarry owners in the Somerset and West Wiltshire area around Bath and Corsham, was later to lead to vast changes at Portland. As was the custom on the Island, land was often divided within a family upon death, this practice leading to some very small plots as the years went by. This ideally suited the Bath company, which had a policy of infiltration by the purchase or lease of land from islanders who had inherited it. It also acquired Government land and land from existing companies.

During 1888 the Bath company obtained a foothold on Portland by the purchase of stone from local quarry owner B.C. White, and in 1898 it acquired the quarries of W.H.P. Weston and appointed a local manager. In the same year it acquired a considerable interest in the John Pearce Stone Company, with the purchase of shares from a Mr Shellabear of Plymouth, who was a major shareholder in John Pearce.

By the turn of the century four companies (excluding the Admiralty) were responsible for producing the majority of stone. Steward & Company, who owned both quarries and a stone cutting works, had a London yard connected by rail at Nine Elms, their own wharf, and a fleet of vessels supplying a considerable trade both within the United Kingdom and in Europe. John Pearce Stone Company, at the time one of the largest in the country, operated quarries and a masonry yard producing around 14,000 tons annually. F.J.Barnes & Company operated a number of quarries and had a modern masonry yard situated alongside Portland station. Weston Quarries, producing between 20,000 and 25,000 tons of stone a year, had a rail-connected yard at Nine Elms, London. By that time the masonry trade was well established on the Island, and supplied a huge amount of finished stone for Government buildings.

The expansion of the Bath Company commenced in August 1900 with the purchase of the old established company of Steward's for a price of £76,000. In 1904 Webber & Pangborne sold their Easton Stone Sawmills and Bottomcombe Masonry Works to the Bath company for £4,750.

By 1911 the latter had become the principal quarry owner on Portland, and it was reconstituted as 'The Bath & Portland Stone Firms Company Limited'. Expansion continued with the acquisition of land from both the Lano and Hodder families in 1915, and the following year the company became lessees of nearly all the Admiralty quarries. In 1920 Admiralty land at Cheyne was purchased, and both quarries and land worked by the Ham Hill & Doulting Stone Company at Headlands (the Grove) was also taken over by Bath & Portland.

Following World War I the use of convict labour ceased in the Admiralty quarries, the final breakwater work having been completed by 1908. The convicts' other main work had been the reconstruction in stone of their own prison, which was completed in 1910, and the supplying of stone for Government work in general. The last Admiralty quarry closed in 1936, after which all requirements were put out to contract.

The formation of the War Graves Commission was to provide a steady trade for stone and masonry products in the following years, a new company, Messrs Smith & Lander (later the Easton Masonry Company), being formed to undertake much of the work. The final large takeover by the Bath & Portland company took place in January 1934 when the yards and quarries of F.J. Barnes were acquired, although the name continued in use until World War II.

By 1939 most of the small private quarries had disappeared, the other large company on the Island being the South Western Stone Company, which had originally commenced operation on Portland in 1909 as the United Stone Company. It also owned quarries in the Somerset, Wiltshire and the Gloucestershire areas, and had a friendly relationship with the Bath Stone Firms. 'United' had a history of financial difficulties, and in 1926 it was reconstituted with new management as United Stone Firms (1926) Ltd. Unfortunately these measures failed in those difficult times, resulting in the sale of the company for £44,000 to the South Western Stone Company in September 1931, the latter having recently been formed from the masonry side of Messrs Higgs & Hills, Civil Engineering Contractors.

It was not until 1960 that the next major upheaval took place, this involving the amalgamation of the Bath & Portland Stone Firms and the South Western Stone Company to form 'The Stone Firms Limited'. By then the large demands for stone had diminished, and what for years had been described as the staple industry was no longer the Island's major employer.

Commemorative stone block placed at the site of the original Priory Corner during 1997 to mark the site of the 'Merchants' Railway'.   *Author*

Chapter Two

The Portland Railway Company
(The 'Merchants' Railway')

The 'Merchants' Railway', locally known as the 'Freemans Incline', was operated by the Portland Railway Company and built solely for the transport of stone.

In the early part of the 19th century demand for Portland stone continued to increase, largely for the construction of Government buildings. The stone exported from the Island during 1824 was no less than 27,000 tons, and it was becoming clear to the quarry owners and the stone merchants alike that serious consideration had to be given to a safer and more efficient way of conveying that material from the top of the Island to a point at sea level where it could be loaded onto sailing vessels. The loading point would have to be in a sheltered place by virtue of the bulky and heavy loads that had to be heaved aboard.

So it was that during 1824 a number of quarry owners, London stone merchants, and other interested parties met to discuss the idea of a railway or tramway to transport the stone to a safe embarkation point. A decision was quickly reached, it being realised that the stone could be moved at very low cost by means of a public railway, and as a result the Portland Railway Company was formed.

Plans were drawn up for the construction of a railway on the north side of the Island. This was to run along a ledge at the top of the Island, eastwards from a point now known as Priory Corner to curve around the edge of what is now the base of the earthworks of the Verne Fort. From there it would descend to sea level near Portland Castle by means of a 586 yds-long inclined plane. It is recorded that by November 1824 the sum of £5 8s. 6d. had been expended on lithographic drawings and printing for the project.

Unlike many early tramways and industrial railways of this period, the proprietors went to Parliament to obtain an Act for the construction of their line, and this was obtained on 10th June, 1825, thus making it a public company. The preamble of the Act set out the company's aims as follows:

> Whereas the making and maintaining of a railway or tramway for the passage of waggons and other carriages from certain lands called Priory Lands . . . to the stone piers near Portland Castle, on the northern coast of the said Island . . . would afford a cheaper conveyance for stone from the stone quarries of the said Island, and would tend to the improvement of the estates in the vicinity of the said railway or tramway, and in other respects be of public utility . . .

The proprietors named in the Act were Gabriel Tucker Steward, Richard Augustus Steward, Rebecca Steward, John Charles Tucker Steward, The Reverend Edward Tucker Steward, Robert Browne, Thomas Richardson the younger, George Frampton, Richard Lano, Hall Wake, Thomas Benjamin Hatchard, Thomas Dike, Bartholomew Comben, George Buckham and John Searle.

ANNO SEXTO

GEORGII IV. REGIS.

..·*****·*··*·**·*****·*·*·*·**·*·**·*******·**·*****·*·**·***·*·**·**

Cap. cxxi.

An Act for making and maintaining a Railway or Tramroad in the Parish of *Saint George*, in the Island of *Portland*, in the County of *Dorset*.
[10th *June* 1825.]

WHEREAS the making and maintaining of a Railway or Tramroad for the Passage of Waggons and other Carriages from certain Lands called *The Priory Lands*, within the Island of *Portland* in the County of *Dorset*, through and over the same, and other Lands and common or commonable Grounds, to the Stone Piers near *Portland Castle*, on the Northern Coast of the said Island, all situate in the Parish of *Saint George* in the said Island, would afford a cheaper Conveyance for Stone from the Stone Quarries of the said Island, and would tend to the Improvement of the Estates in the Vicinity of the said Railway or Tramroad, and in other respects be of public Utility : And whereas the several Persons herein-after named are desirous at their own Costs and Charges to make and maintain such Railway or Tramroad, but the same cannot be effected without the Aid and Authority of Parliament : May it therefore please Your Majesty that it may be enacted ; and be it enacted by the King's most Excellent Majesty, by and with the Advice and Consent of the Lords Spiritual and Temporal, and Commons, in this present Parliament assembled, and by the Authority of the same, That *Gabriel Tucker Steward, Richard Augustus Tucker Steward, Rebecca Steward, John Charles Tucker Steward,* the Reverend *Edward Tucker Steward, Robert Browne, Thomas Richardson*

Proprietors incorporated

[*Local.*]   35 N

Act of Parliament 1825 for the Portland Railway. The first Act of Parliament for the construction of a railway in the County of Dorset.

The seal of the Portland Railway Company.   *Author's Collection*

Another factor that made the line unusual from many other and later railways was that the company had no financial problems. The estimated cost of the line was £4,689 12s., and even before the Bill went to Parliament £5,000 had already been subscribed by several persons, thus enabling the work to commence just as soon as the Bill received the Royal Assent.

The design and construction of the line was entrusted to Mr James Brown, a civil engineer, but the ink was hardly dry on the Act of Parliament before the company found itself in trouble with Captain Augustus Manning, the Governor of Portland Castle. In August Captain Manning complained, 'The persons who ship stone on the west side of the Castle have obstructed the free course of the water from the ditch, and have affected the drainage of the Castle by a wharf in its vicinity, and what was formerly the ditch of the Castle on this side is now converted into a road for shipping stone'. He further stated that an Act of Parliament laid down that no building was to be erected within 200 yards of the Castle, and he was therefore most displeased to find that preparations were being made for the building of a branch of this railway to the piers on the west side of the Castle. This would pass quite close to the walls, and thereby obstruct the entrance to carriages.

As a result of this complaint John Searle, of the Portland Railway Company, received a letter from 'The men at the Ministry' (known then as The Crown Commissioners of Woods & Forests), referring to the encroachment on the wastes of the Isle of Portland that had been complained of to the Board of

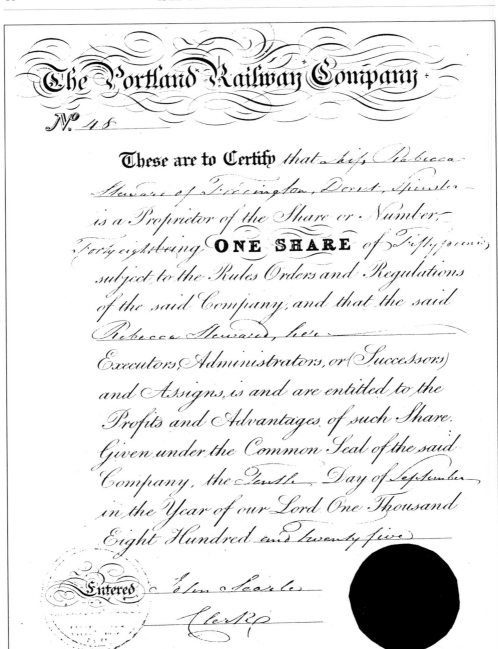

The Portland Railway Company

Nº 48

These are to Certify that *Miss Rebecca Steward of Torrington, Dorset, Spinster* is a Proprietor of the Share or Number, *Forty eight* being **ONE SHARE** of *Fifty pounds*, subject to the Rules Orders and Regulations of the said Company, and that the said *Rebecca Steward, her* Executors, Administrators, or (Successors) and Assigns, is and are entitled to the Profits and Advantages of such Share. Given under the Common Seal of the said Company, the *Tenth* Day of *September* in the Year of our Lord One Thousand Eight Hundred *and twenty five*

Entered *John Searle*

Clerk

Portland Railway Co. share certificate, 1825.

Ordnance, 'with a view to getting removed the obstruction that now existed to the defence of the Castle'. It suggested that the piers on the west side of the building be re-sited on the east side which, they observed, would not only enable them to add to the defence of the Castle, but would also be of advantage to the proprietors of the quarries.

Several letters passed between the parties concerned in the argument, each defending their own case, until a certain Roger Hawkins arrived at Portland to survey the 'Railroad Encroachments'. Existing records are somewhat vague as to how agreement was reached, but the piers were eventually built on the east side of the Castle, and it seems that Hawkins was then employed by the Portland Railway Company in the position of a consultant, for in July 1829 he sent the company a bill for £630 9s. 0d. for his part in laying out and superintending the making of the railway.

In July 1825 Mr Hall Wake, Chairman of the Portland Railway Company, received a letter from a Shropshire ironmaster offering to supply waggons and other materials, but he wrote that he had his doubts about which system the company was going to use for the conveyance of such heavy loads. However, work on the construction of the line went ahead very quickly, and it was opened to traffic by October 1826. In the short period between then and 31st December that year 4,803 tons of stone had been carried over the line to give a net income of £289 2s. 1½d., although there had been some delay to traffic and operational teething troubles resulting from inexperience with this mode of transport.

With the railway operational stone could travel down the steep north face of Portland to the sheltered piers in the lee of the Island, and it would be as well at this point to discuss the method of working the railway during the early part of its existence. The stone was brought to Priory Corner from the quarries in horse-drawn carts, being transferred by crane at that point onto the waggons of the 'Merchants' Railway'. The little trains of 4 ft 6 in. gauge waggons were then hitched to a team of horses which proceeded to haul them along the hillside ledge, over the level crossing of what is now known as Verne Hill Road, then around the side of Verne Hill from the head of Tillycombe to the top drum of the incline railway. This was situated just below a point where the road to the north entrance of what is now the Verne Prison crossed the line on a steel bridge.

There were no engines or other power-operated machinery to haul the loaded and empty trucks up and down the steeply graded incline, the whole system relying solely on a counter balance method of operation. To balance the load on its way down, a sufficient number of empty waggons had to be attached at the bottom of the incline to travel up. In practice this meant that a suitable number of empty waggons had always to be on hand at the foot of the incline in order that the system could operate. On reaching the top drum the horses were unhitched and the waggons were lowered down the first incline on the end of a chain wound several times around the drum. Speed was controlled by the weight of the empty waggons being hauled up on the other end of the chain, there also being a brake on the drum to assist control.

The drum was of timber construction with the winding gear mounted on a framework. This first inclined plane - from the top to a short level section - was

303 yards in length. At this midway point there was another drum similar in construction to the top one, and the same procedure was adopted. The waggons were attached to another chain and lowered down the final 282 yards to sea level, where a further team of horses hauled them across what is now Castle Road to the piers on the east side of Portland Castle. On arrival at the piers the stone was unloaded into ships for transportation to its destination or nearest sea port.

This, then, was the line of the Portland Railway Company. Quarry owners subsequently laid private lines from Priory Corner into their quarries on the west side of the Island, and at various times short inclines were constructed from the quarries at Yeates to meet the company's line. In the early days an incline ran down the present south entrance of the Verne Prison to meet the 'Merchants' at the top of Tillycombe.

Shortly after the opening of the line, Mr Hall Wake wrote to Mr Searle to say that he had looked at the system and found that eight more waggons were required to keep it working, delays being experienced at the drums because there were insufficient waggons to balance the loads.

On 1st January, 1827 an agreement was signed between one James Brown and the Portland Railway Company under which Brown was authorised to load stone brought to Priory Corner, or any part of the system, and deliver the same. He was authorised to take over 17 waggons, two of which were damaged and had to be repaired.

Damage frequently occurred on the line, and a letter from Brown to Searle dated 18th January, 1827 described how the chain on the lower incline parted and in doing so broke 6 wheels, 1 axle, 14 plates and pedestals and damaged two waggons. The flimsy nature of the chain was suspected as the cause, and a replacement ⅒th inch larger in diameter was suggested.

The length of the chains are quoted as:

4 yards around the barrel of the drum.
10 yards from the drum to the top of the incline.
303 yards down the first inclined plane. (282 yds down the second inclined plane.)
4 yards on the flat at the bottom.

On 17th July, 1827, the Chairman of the Portland Railway Company, Hall Wake of Millbank Street, Westminster, died. He was a London stone merchant who had been one of the instigators in getting the line constructed.

More troubles on the line occurred in January 1828 when a large landslip, 80 square yards in extent, occurred at the lower drum. The slip broke a frame brace and blocked the track. It took eight men two weeks to clear, but the company managed to keep the railway open despite the existence at the same time of another slip in the cutting near the foot of the incline at Castletown.

A meeting was arranged at Abingdon Street, Westminster, on 8th March, 1827, but this was not attended by sufficient proprietors and was postponed until 12th April, when it was again a failure through lack of support.

A letter of the period stated: 'The Railway is very disheartening, and the Company begin to despair of ever getting out of debt', and this must have been the general consensus of opinion amongst the proprietors. They obviously did not want to hear more bad news, for further meetings arranged for 11th July, 1831 and 4th June, 1832 were not supported and were also cancelled.

During 1835 the line came under new management when Messrs Robert Spencer and William Lowman took over the running of the railway from James Brown. This resulted in an increase in business, for the following year 32,315 tons of stone travelled over the line, bringing in a revenue of £1,232 1s. 9d.

Stone quarrying and hauling was hard and dangerous work, and accidents inevitably happened. Such was the case of John Mears, who lost an arm whilst employed on the railway. During 1840 he was given a donation of £10 from his employers, and later received another £5 from them. In 1843 he made a request for further assistance and was given another £5 - but this time unwillingly, for the company Chairman was requested to explain to Mears that he was not now employed by them, and that he must consider the former payments as donations and not as a pension by right. However, in the following year (1844), Mears asked once more for assistance, and received another £5.

The line had now got into a bad state of repair, and a contractor was called in. One-hundred-and-one new rollers and pedestals for the guidance of the chain were ordered, and in June 1844 the contractor reported that the general condition of the line was deplorable. Many of the stone blocks that had been laid by the original contractor, James Brown, were too small and were giving a great deal of trouble. The railway company agreed that new blocks should be purchased as required at its expense, but insisted they were laid at the expense of the contractor.

By June 1845 there was still no marked improvement in the affairs of the line, so the Portland Railway Company decided to take over the working of the line itself instead of contracting out. A committee of management was appointed, consisting of Roper Weston, Benjamin Scriven, William Lock, William White, and Johnathan Lano. One Thomas Sansom was employed as foreman at a wage of £1 per week. The committee was given the powers to purchase any horses required and to employ carters, general workmen, and boys, and also to purchase tools and contract for the supply of hay and corn. It was also decreed that after 30th June no waggon would be permitted to leave the company's line without the permission of three members of the committee.

The committee idea failed, and by February 1845 the running of the line was once again contracted out - this time to Richard Lano, who purchased the horses and harness from the company at valuation price.

In 1853 the merchants were complaining to the railway of delays in the delivery of stone. Mr Lano's explanation was that there was a shortage of waggons caused by the merchants themselves who were taking the company's waggons into the quarries. It was therefore ruled that its trucks were not to be taken into the quarries, unless the merchants involved supplied an equal number of waggons in return to keep the inclines working efficiently.

By the following year (1854) Mr Lano had become disenchanted with the price he was being paid for hauling, and made the suggestion that he be paid 6½d. per ton, but the company could not afford to pay so much and offered him 6d. per ton.

There was another demand for money in May 1854 when a claim was received from Phillip Dodson for £28 1s. 6d. in respect of a quantity of stone that

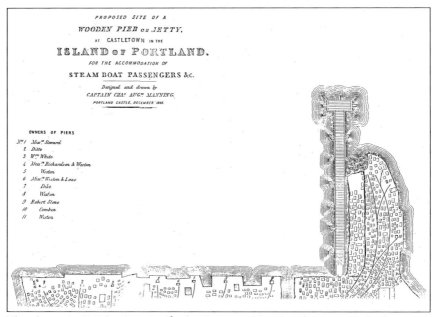

Plan drawn in 1848 by Captain Charles Augustus Manning, for a pier at Castletown to accommodate the paddle steamers operating from Weymouth. In the event a pier at an angle was constructed. The drawing clearly shows the loading points occupied by each stone merchant, in this the original layout.

had been lost on the railway. Apparently the stone had been inadvertently dispatched to Mr Weston's pier and shipped out to an unknown destination!

The framework of the two incline winding drums had deteriorated, and they were now in a very bad state of repair. It was therefore agreed that a roof be built over them to give some protection from the elements. The work was undertaken by a Mr Handsford during the summer of 1854 at a cost of £25 14s. 8d.

Mr Lano was still not satisfied with the price per ton he was receiving for haulage, so at a general meeting held at the Portland Arms Hotel on 20th March, 1855 he resigned his contract and a tender from James Dike was accepted by the Board.

Meanwhile, urgent minor repairs were not receiving due attention, with the result that when they became absolutely essential they proved very expensive. Because of this another committee was formed in April, its task being to inspect the railway and plant every six months and ensure that remedial action could be taken before defects became too serious.

Before long Mr Dike found that the financial rewards of running the railway were becoming increasingly elusive, and he soon requested an additional penny a ton to haul the stone, otherwise, he said, he would be forced to end his contract. This threat did him no good, for the company accepted his resignation, and tenders were put out for another contractor. When Dike realised that his ultimatum had not had the desired affect and that a new contractor was being sought, he immediately put in another tender offering to haul the stone for ½d. a ton more, for which he would also undertake to put the trucks and railway into good order. As a result he was allowed to remain in office, at least until his original contract expired.

In the early part of the 19th century men had to work extremely hard to earn a living, and many remained in harness to their employers until they dropped. It is therefore interesting to note that when the proprietors of the Portland Railway Company were informed in 1885 that Henry Gibbs, who had been clerk at the top drum for the past 35 years, had become ill and was unable to perform his duties, the company retired him and resolved to pay him a pension of 5s. per week.

In 1859 new pedestals and rollers were ordered from the firm of James Cox, but at a meeting held on 24th October the proprietors were told the order was then 35 days late in delivery. The terms of Mr Cox's contract imposed a penalty clause of £1 per day if delivery was not made by the stipulated date, and unfortunately for Cox the meeting decided to implement the penalty.

A new regulation for the working of the line was introduced at this meeting, it being ruled that in order to keep the track in good repair, no waggon could be used upon it with less than 1 inch or more than 1½ inches of flange on each wheel.

With a good and steady trade in progress a failure of either the railway or the drums could cause serious delays and loss of revenue - but by now much of the equipment was beginning to show signs of its age. At a meeting on 18th January, 1860, the Directors were told that a loan had been secured from Peter Swatridge of Weymouth, amounting to £500 at 5 per cent per annum interest, and this would enable the upper part of the railway to be put into good order. The meeting also decided that a traffic manager be appointed to look after the day-to-day running of the line, and to inspect the stock using it.

By this time the two incline drums were in poor condition. The chains had caused great problems from the start, and as far back as 1857 their replacement with wire ropes had been considered, but the existing drums were only 6 ft in diameter and a wire rope required a drum with a diameter of not less than 12 ft to work efficiently. Consequently at that time no more had been done, but now the situation had become serious and some urgent action was needed. A meeting was convened at the Portland Arms Hotel in March 1860 to discuss the best course of action, one suggestion being to dispense with the two drums altogether and join the two inclines by means of a short embankment at the site of the lower drum to form one continuous incline. At the top there was to be a brake wheel so designed as to enable wire ropes to be used. The meeting approved this scheme, adding that at the same time the smith's shop at the top of the upper incline should be removed and a siding laid on the site. At a meeting on 18th April, 1860 Mr Coode, the engineer of the Portland Breakwater project (then under construction), was given permission to lay a single line of rails alongside the 'Merchants' Railway' at Castletown. This was required to carry stone to a site in Castletown, and for this privilege he was to be charged a wayleave of 2d. per ton for stone travelling westwards and 1d. per ton for stone travelling eastwards. Other business at the meeting included the appointment

PORTLAND RAILWAY.

TO BE SOLD

BY AUCTION,

BY MR. POTHECARY,

At the Golden Lion Hotel, in Weymouth,

On MONDAY, the 9th day of FEB., 1863,

Precisely at Four o'clock in the Afternoon,

TEN SHARES

OF

£50 EACH,

IN THE

PORTLAND RAILWAY,

In 5 Lots of 2 Shares each, or such others as may be agreed upon at the time of Sale.

The Dividends on the above Shares have been usually at the rate of 10 per cent. per annum, and the Traffic is now steadily increasing.

For further particulars apply to the AUCTIONEER, or to

MR. TEMPLER, Solicitor,

BRIDPORT.

Dated, 7th January, 1863.

J. SHERREN, PRINTER, WEYMOUTH.

Auction notice for the sale of shares in the Portland Railway Company dated February 1863.

Author's Collection

of Benjamin Pearce as traffic manager. It was also resolved that a fine of £2 be imposed on any stone merchant who used waggons on the railway which were not in a good state of repair.

The improved method of working the line was operating well, but during an inspection in 1863 there was found to be considerable wear in the wire rope then in use. Mr Holland was consulted about the matter, with the result that he ordered a quantity of India rubber bands that were to be wound around the wheels of the machinery, thereby reducing the friction on the wire rope.

In 1864 Mr Holland suggested the construction of a second line of railway at the bottom of the incline to assist in the flow of waggons to the loading piers, thus increasing the efficiency of the railway. This work was quickly put in hand and resulted in an increased flow of stone, the tonnage carried in 1866 amounting to 70,888 which brought in a revenue of £2,909 19s. 8d.

The opening of the Weymouth & Portland Railway in 1865 enabled an exchange point with the 'Merchants' Railway' to be introduced, a pair of sidings at Castletown, reached by a short branch from Portland station, being situated near the foot of the incline. The non-standard gauge of 4 ft 6½ in. in use on the 'Merchants' line prevented the operation of main line stock on the system, but in any case the state of the permanent way left a lot to be desired, and fell far short of normal railway standards.

Traffic on the railway increased so rapidly thereafter that, in February 1866, the Directors decided that the line from the top of the incline to the edge of a field belonging to Mr Lano should be doubled to cater for the expanding trade. It was also suggested that a charge of 2s. should be made for goods travelling up the incline.

One of the extensions to the railway had to be moved to a new site around this time. Owing to construction work taking place in connection with the Verne fortifications, the short incline with a brake drum which ran down from what later became the Verne's South Gate to the main line at the head of Tillycombe was in the way. In its reconstructed form it became the incline running from New Ground down under the three bridges to the main line.

In March 1867 it was proposed that a competent person be engaged as manager of the railway, the Directors deciding to contact the Army Pensions Employment Society with a view to engaging a suitable man. The result of this enquiry was realised the following month, for in April a Mr Wildman, formerly a sergeant in the Sappers and Miners, was accepted for the post at a weekly wage of £1 5s. 0d. Labourers on the line at that time were receiving a daily wage of between 3s. and 3s. 6d.

After taking up his appointment Wildman soon made his presence felt by making many alterations in an effort to smarten up operations. In 1868 Wildman reported that the horse employed at the top of the incline was no longer fit for the work required of it, and a younger animal was purchased for the job. On the death of Benjamin Pearce in 1869 Wildman was appointed traffic manager in addition to his post as Manager of the railway, his weekly wage being increased by 5s. to £1 10s. During the construction of the Verne Fort a section of company land was sold to the Ordnance Department for the sum of £1,250, the Directors deciding that £1,200 of the money should be distributed equally amongst the

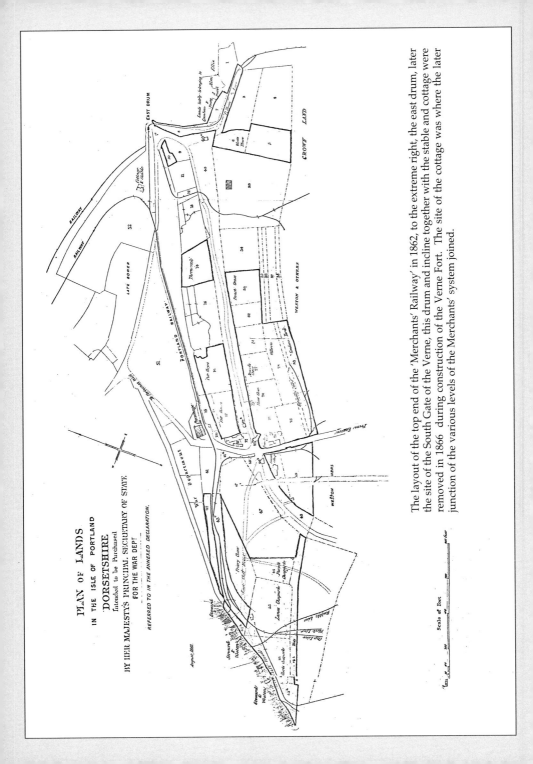

PLAN of LANDS
IN THE ISLE OF PORTLAND
DORSETSHIRE
Intended to be Purchased
BY HER MAJESTY'S PRINCIPAL SECRETARY OF STATE
FOR THE WAR DEP.T

REFERRED TO IN THE ANNEXED DECLARATION.

August 1860.

Scale of Feet

EAST DRUM

RAILWAY

LATE BOWER

CROWN LAND

WESTON & OTHERS

WESTON

HERS

PORTLAND RAILWAY

The layout of the top end of the 'Merchants' Railway' in 1862, to the extreme right, the east drum, later the site of the South Gate of the Verne, this drum and incline together with the stable and cottage were removed in 1866 during construction of the Verne Fort. The site of the cottage was where the later junction of the various levels of the Merchants' system joined.

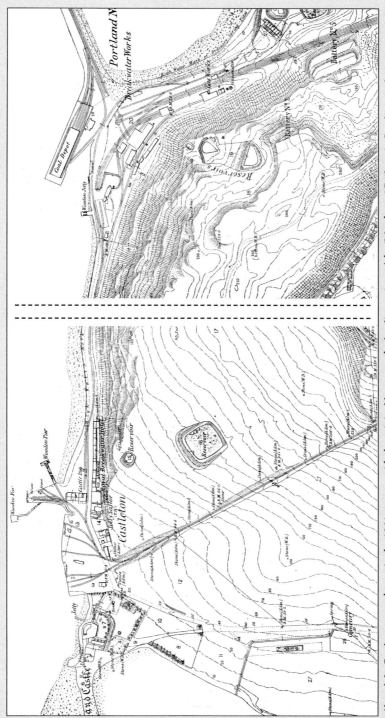

Above left: Castletown as shown in the 1864 survey, with the original layout at the loading points of the 'Merchants' Railway'. One line can be seen running to the right towards the breakwater works, although owing to the difference in gauge there was no physical connection between the two systems.
Above right: The Breakwater works as shown in the same survey, by which time considerable development had taken place.

(Both) Reproduced from the 25″, 1864 Ordnance Survey Map

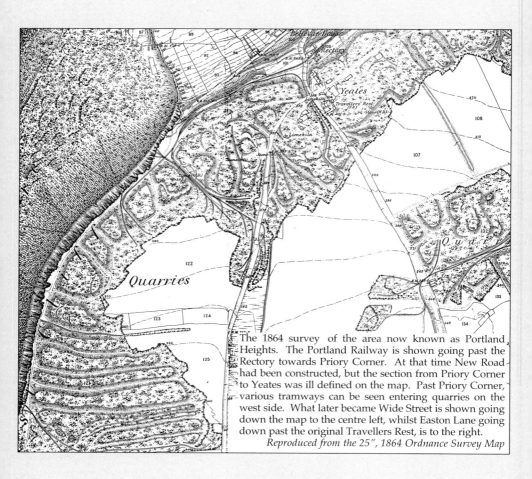

The 1864 survey of the area now known as Portland Heights. The Portland Railway is shown going past the Rectory towards Priory Corner. At that time New Road had been constructed, but the section from Priory Corner to Yeates was ill defined on the map. Past Priory Corner, various tramways can be seen entering quarries on the west side. What later became Wide Street is shown going down the map to the centre left, whilst Easton Lane going down past the original Travellers Rest, is to the right.

Reproduced from the 25″, 1864 Ordnance Survey Map

An early engraving first published about 1851, showing the original middle drum of the incline.

One of the earliest known photographs of the Portland Railway taken during the 1850s. The incline shown with the overhead drum ran from the present site of the South Gate of the Verne, to its junction with the main line running from Priory Corner, shown extreme right with loaded wagon. The line to the left ran around the west face of Verne Hill before descending the main incline to Castletown. With the construction of the Verne Fort both the building in the foreground and the incline were removed.

Author's Collection

A view taken at the end of the Great War of the same area as shown in the previous photograph. In the background the completed works of the Verne Fort in the South Gate area. The road in the foreground leading to the South Gate is crossed by the Portland Railway line from Priory Corner, further up the road can be seen the parapets of the bridge crossing the incline from Yeates. The two Australian soldiers in the photograph were stationed at the Verne at that period.   *Author's Collection*

The various levels of the Portland Railway can be seen in this view from the top of Tillycombe. The main line from Priory Corner crosses on the bridge in the centre. The top bridge carries the 'top road' to the South Gate of the Verne and the bottom inclined bridge carries the road from Fortuneswell to the South Gate of the Verne. Down the centre is the cable-operated incline from Yeates Quarries, this being constructed to replace the earlier incline to the east, removed to allow construction of the South Gate of the Verne. The brake drum is visible under the top arch. The waggon at the bottom is just joining the lower main line from Priory Corner which comes in from the right.   *Author's Collection*

Yeates incline, empty waggons begin the ascent, and loaded wagons the descent. At the top, the overhead brake drum is clearly shown, note the common centre rail and the arrangements at the passing point. Of particular interest is the unusual point blade at the foot of the incline to serve the centre rail.
K. Bakes Collection

Looking up Yeates incline, the overhead drum at the top being clearly shown. Halfway up the incline the passing loop is visible, as are the rope and guide rollers.   *Author's Collection*

A general view taken from Priory Corner after the Great War. In the foreground the horses, wagons, crane and building used by the 'Merchants' Railway'. Behind is Fortuneswell to the right, Chiswell to the left, the curve of the railway at Portland station is clearly shown. Behind lay the oil tanks and Portland Harbour. *Author's Collection*

With their heads in their nose bags, a four horsepower train is about to depart from Priory Corner on its journey to the top of the incline. The crude construction of the waggons and the insecure loading of the stone is clearly visible. *E. Latcham Collection*

Horses pulling away from Priory Corner with a load of stone heading for Castletown. Note the 'point blade' arrangement in the bottom right-hand corner. *Author's Collection*

Looking eastwards down on the main line of the Portland Railway, towards the the Verne, the earthworks of which can be seen above the Rectory in the foreground. The two lines of the railway can be seen cut into the side of the earthworks. The archway facing the top line housed the head of a fresh water spring, situated in the outer wall of the Verne Ditch which dropped down between the top and second set of raised earthworks. *Author's Collection*

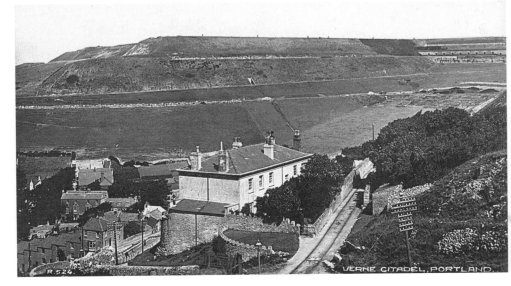

shareholders in accordance with the number of shares held by each, and £50 kept to one side to cover any expenses that may have been incurred in the deal.

A great deal of mechanical failure on the railway was still being caused by waggons in poor condition. On 16th January, 1869 a truck belonging to Mr W.H.P. Weston broke away from the drum, causing considerable damage to the line. Mr Weston denied liability, but agreed to abide by the findings of an arbitrator. An enquiry was set up, presided over by John Coode, the result being that Mr Weston was found to have been at fault by using a defective truck, and he was ordered to pay £79 3s. 7d. to repair the damage caused.

Mr Wildman was a keen and conscientious man who worked well for the company. To his way of thinking rules were made to be obeyed, and in the early part of 1871 he marked trucks belonging to the Portland Stone Company as unfit for use on the line, the wheels being in poor condition, but that company still persisted in running the condemned waggons. However, at a railway company meeting in March of the same year Mr Foot (the Secretary) was instructed to write to the stone firm involved, stressing in no uncertain terms the regulations regarding the use of the company's metals.

At a further meeting on 27th July the Portland Stone Company once again found itself in trouble, this time Mr Foot reporting that several accounts with the firm remained outstanding, including one for £231 9s. 1d. The meeting resolved that the Portland Stone Company be requested to remove, at its own expense, all trucks not in immediate use that were standing on the 'Merchants' Railway'.

All was not well within the Portland Railway Company itself, as a general meeting held at the Portland Arms Hotel on 2nd April, 1872 revealed. Mr Foot, the Secretary, had tendered his resignation, and the gathering was soon to find out why! His place was taken by Mr B. Hopkins at a salary of £25 per annum, which included his travelling expenses between Weymouth and Portland.

Mr Foot's accounts and cash books were laid before the meeting, and an extract from the minutes of that meeting will explain the reason.

'It would appear for years past Mr Foot has omitted to enter monies received, and has made mistakes casting up the receipts etc. showing that since the year 1865 the Company has been defrauded of the sum of £783 3s. 7d.' Now the facts were known, the Board had to decide on a course of action, for a tremendous amount of cash was involved. It was eventually resolved that Mr Hopkins, the new Secretary, would write to Foot and inform him that the company was anxious if at all possible to avoid taking legal action against him, but that it expected - and in fact required - a payment of cash against the admitted deficit as shown in the books. The company also demanded a true statement of his personal affairs so that they would be in a position to judge the degree of forbearance they might be inclined to show him.

On receipt of the details of Foot's means another meeting was called on 23rd July at which it was decided to inform the former Secretary that he should endeavour to arrange for the transfer of the lease of his house in Clapham Road, London, to the Portland Railway Company against the admitted defalcation. No doubt this affair made Foot a very sick man, for he died on 7th March, 1873 before any of the cash could be repaid. On hearing the news of his demise, a special meeting was called on 16th April to discuss the situation. Mr Foot's son now held the lease of his father's

Two loaded waggons await departure from the top of the incline. After moving forward they will be connected to the cable and proceed down the incline to the left of the picture. The building housing the brake drum is just ahead of the waggons.   *Author's Collection*

With the assistance of a crowbar loaded waggons begin their descent of the 'Merchants' incline.
J.H. Lucking Collection

property in London, the transfer of which to the Portland Railway Company had not yet been effected, and as there was no will the situation became complicated. However, Mr Foot Jr stated that he was prepared to pay the sum of £100, which would consist of £50 cash in two instalments at three and six months towards the liquidation of his father's debts provided no further action was taken, and this was accepted. To ensure a situation like this could never occur again, the Portland company decided to appoint Auditors to keep a tight check on the accounts.

In August 1874, Mr Bristowe, Solicitor to the Admiralty, wrote to the Portland Railway requesting permission to erect a bridge across the 'Merchants' Railway' at Castletown, as it was intended to link the Breakwater railway with the Weymouth & Portland line. The Portland Railway Company put this matter into the hands of Peter Bruff, a civil engineer from Ipswich, requesting him to inspect the Admiralty's plans and to investigate the terms. A further letter from Bristowe stated that the Admiralty could give no guarantees over terms, as this new section of line was to be constructed for them jointly by the Great Western and London & South Western Railway companies, and it was therefore with those two bodies that the Portland railway should correspond. However, agreement was reached between the two parties concerned and the construction of the bridge went ahead as planned. But its completion created a slight problem because it obstructed the view that the incline brakeman previously had from the top to the bottom of the incline, making it extremely difficult for him to control the system safely. This called for the provision of a signalling system, a semaphore arm being erected at the lower end of the incline in a position where it could be clearly seen above the new bridge. A hut to give shelter to the operator during inclement weather was also provided, the total cost being £19 4s. 5d. The Great Western Railway (on behalf of the joint companies) paid the signalman's wages for the period up to the 30th June, 1876.

It was not until December 1880 that the Portland Railway Company received from the GWR and LSWR companies the sum of £250 in respect of the bridge. By the time the solicitors' fees and a gratuity to Mr Hopkins for his services in obtaining the agreed terms had been deducted the Portland Railway made only £55 2s. 1d. from the deal.

However, in 1874 the Directors considered a scheme to upgrade the railway and alter the gauge to 4ft 8½ in., together with the remodelling of the curves and points to enable wagons of the GWR and LSWR to run over the line to gain direct access to the quarries. Part of the scheme involved lighting the railway with gas lamps to allow the company to work additional hours, but nothing ever came of this. In fact, all that did happen was an increase in the charges for transporting goods up the incline from 3½d. to 6d. per ton from 1st July, 1876.

John Wildman, superintendent of the line, died during the summer of 1880, and at a company meeting held on 30th September the Directors granted his widow a gratuity of £5 in appreciation of the services rendered by her late husband. Two years later, in July 1882, the company received a letter from Mrs Wildman stating that she was in very distressed circumstances, and asking for help. The company sent her £1, but pointed out that she had no claim on it and intimated that no further help would be given. William Millish was appointed to the late Mr Wildman's position at a wage of £1 5s. per week.

Portland. Quarry Railway.

Loaded waggons proceeding down the incline towards Portland Harbour. In the foreground are the cables and guide rollers, and in the middle distance the passing loop.

Author's Collection

A view looking up the incline from under the Easton Railway Bridge. The common centre rail ran throughout the incline, except for a short passing loop.   *Author's Collection*

A pre-World War I view taken at the bottom of the incline. Behind the workmen is the new bridge carrying the Easton & Church Hope Railway, and the footbridge to the Royal Naval Hospital. The semaphore signal used to control the incline is clearly shown. Under the bridge loaded wagons have arrived, whilst empty wagons stand in the foreground awaiting the return journey, other loaded wagons stand in a siding.   *Author's Collection*

A postcard view of the bottom of the incline, tracks to the left going to Castletown pier and those to the right leading to Castletown sidings. Behind the bridge the semaphore signal stands on the left side, this being used to communicate with the brake drum at the top of the incline.

Author's Collection

Loaded waggons wait at the foot of the incline to be moved either to Castletown sidings or Castletown pier. Just behind the waggons is the bridge carrying the Easton line, and a footbridge leading to the Naval Hospital.   *E. Latcham Collection*

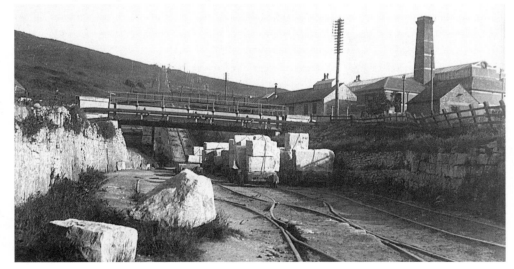

A view looking up the incline in later years. A two-horse team haul loaded waggons away towards Castletown pier, whilst empty waggons await ascent on the left. Just under the bridge, on the right can be seen the hut housing the signalling instrument controlling the working of the incline. *J.H. Lucking Collection*

Another view looking up the incline in later years. *J.H. Lucking Collection*

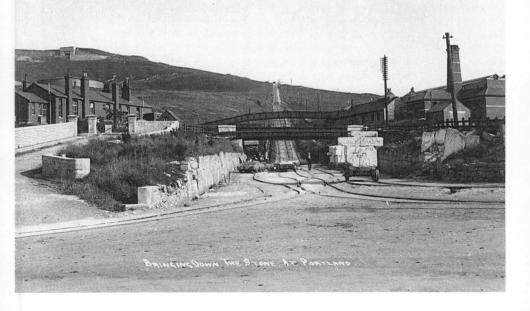

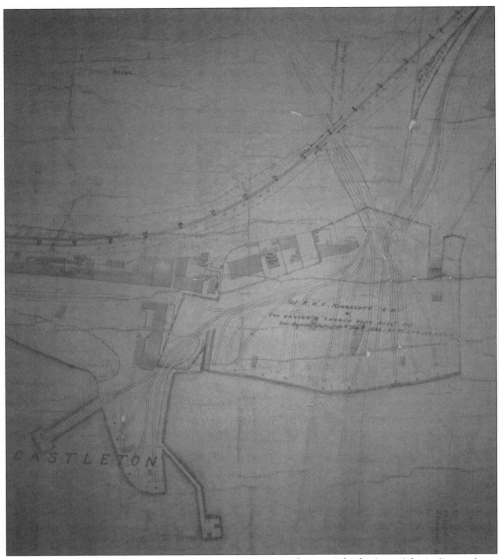

The layout of the loading piers at Castletown in 1873, to the top right the foot of the incline and the transfer sidings with the Weymouth & Portland Railway, to the top left the planned Dockyard Railway. Bottom left, the original Castletown pier, on the right the steam boat jetty, this was removed during the improvements of 1897 when the left side of Castletown pier was enlarged.

Improvements to the railway were again discussed at a meeting held on 23rd August, 1883, when replacement of the horses with steam traction was considered, together with the possibility of extending the line to afford better communication with the pier at Castletown. The upgrading of the railway to cater for passenger traffic was also considered, but when the proposals were put to the vote there were only two in favour and seven against, and the scheme was dropped. One can only admire the Victorians for their optimism; even by the standards of the time there was no possibility that the 'Merchants' Railway' could ever be upgraded to carry passengers, with such a steep gradient and a rope-hauled incline. Indeed even conventional railways of the period were coming under increasing scrutiny by the Board of Trade as to their operating methods.

Also in 1883 the Easton & Church Hope company was still trying desperately to construct its line on the Island, so in December the Portland Railway Company appointed Mr R.N. Howard as the company's Solicitor to keep an eye on the progress of the Easton company. He was to take any steps he considered necessary to protect the interests of the Portland concern, but the cost of his brief was not to exceed £70!

At a general meeting of the Portland Railway Company held on 16th July, 1885, the subject of the Easton & Church Hope line again came to the fore. After the general business had been completed Mr Alt, of the Easton & Church Hope company, was introduced to the gathering. He placed before the meeting an offer to acquire either the whole or the majority of the Portland Railway shares, promising to forward to the Company Secretary the precise terms within one week. The meeting resolved that a copy of the letter and the offer be sent to each shareholder, requesting that each reply to the Secretary individually giving their opinion on the matter.

As promised, Mr Alt's offer on behalf of the Easton & Church Hope company arrived at the Portland Railway office with the suggested terms: the Easton & Church Hope company to acquire the property of the Portland Railway Company at a purchase price of £10,000, consisting of £5,000 in cash and the remaining £5,000 made up of preference shares in the Easton & Church Hope company, but if any of the shareholders so desired, they could receive a cash payment instead of half preference shares.

A general meeting of the Portland Railway Company was held at the Portland Arms Hotel on 27th August to discuss Mr Alt's offer and to vote on it. The voting on the issue could not have been closer, for 38 were in favour of the takeover and 39 against. By this very slender margin Mr Alt lost the day.

The Easton & Church Hope Railway had been formed in 1867 with plans to construct a pier and several short railways to ship stone from the Island in direct competition with the Portland Railway. But the pier was never constructed, and only six furlongs of railway had been built. In 1884 the Easton company obtained powers to construct two more railways on the Island, but this met with the opposition of the Portland Railway Company, and to date the Easton Railway had only constructed 1 mile of its line and no buildings had been erected! With the failure of Mr Alt's bid to take over the Portland Railway, the Easton & Church Hope went to Parliament seeking powers to make a compulsory purchase of the former - including powers to run over both the

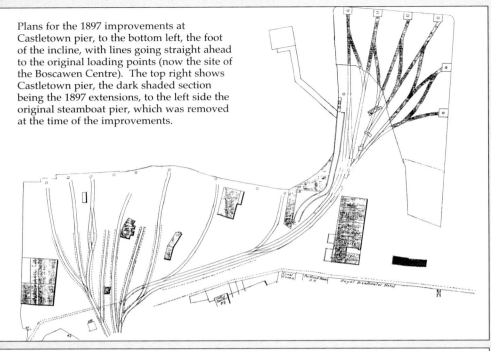

Plans for the 1897 improvements at Castletown pier, to the bottom left, the foot of the incline, with lines going straight ahead to the original loading points (now the site of the Boscawen Centre). The top right shows Castletown pier, the dark shaded section being the 1897 extensions, to the left side the original steamboat pier, which was removed at the time of the improvements.

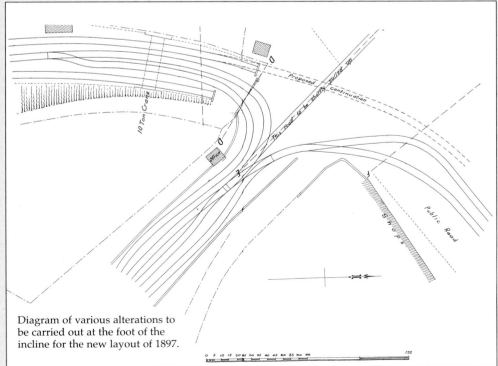

Diagram of various alterations to be carried out at the foot of the incline for the new layout of 1897.

132

Portland company's line and that belonging to Mr Weston, and to alter the gauge of the railway to 4ft 8½ in. The Bill was strongly opposed by both the Portland Railway Company and the quarry owners. The 'Merchants' Railway' had been in operation since 1826 and was a proven success, and Mr Weston and other quarry owners had constructed their own lines to 4 ft 6½ in. gauge in order to make junctions with the 'Merchants' line, and it was argued that any change in this arrangement would disjoint the system and create difficulties to both workers and quarry owners alike. Although the Easton Bill received the Royal Assent for other purposes, the parts relating to the Portland Railway Company were withdrawn, thus saving that company from a difficult situation.

By 1894 the 21 year lease which the Portland Railway Company had taken on land at Castletown was running out, the actual date of expiry being 5th January, 1895. As about half the tonnage carried by the railway was shipped from the piers at Castletown, it must have been realised that urgent action was necessary to protect the company's interest, yet - somewhat oddly - no immediate action was taken on either side even when the date arrived. The lessees, the Commissioners of Woods and Forests, seemed as willing to overlook the expiry of the lease as was the railway, and 10 months passed before a company meeting on 24th October, 1895 appointed a sub-committee to investigate the matter. By then there was a fear that, as the lease had expired for such a length of time, the company could literally have the ground taken from underneath its feet!

During 1853 the Portland Railway had purchased seven strips of land close to the piers from the Commissioners of Woods and Forests, and in 1895 it obtained the freehold on seven sidings. The Board now decided that it would be more beneficial for them to exchange these sidings and land for a new site rather than make a cash settlement on the leasehold land. However the Commissioners were not prepared to offer any exchanges and would only settle for a cash payment of £250 to purchase the sidings, which was in fact less than the company had paid for the land in 1853. In January 1897 the company agreed to accept the £250 figure and to take a 31 year lease at £25 per annum on the land required for the new works.

The construction of the new pier commenced in August 1897, a great advantage to the company being that most of the materials for use in the work could be carried to the site over its own line. The new pier was to the east of the existing structures. It was a large three-sided pier, providing much more working space than had previously existed. Construction work went well, and by the following October the old steamboat pier had been demolished - a task that commenced as soon as the Weymouth paddle steamers concluded their summer services. The whole building programme was completed during December 1898, when Messrs Hills, the contractor, handed everything over to the company.

The pier was now to the east of the incline, which necessitated the laying of an additional section of line to link the two. The new line crossed Castle Road and then ran alongside it for about 100 yards before bearing left onto the pier.

While all this work was being carried out it was decided to implement a scheme (drawn up in 1881) to dispense with the turntable at the foot of the incline, used to gain access to the Weymouth & Portland company's yard at

Castletown Road, with loaded waggon waiting to proceed to the pier which is situated behind the brick building on the left. The lines from the incline lead out of the picture in the bottom right.

Author's Collection

Castletown. Fifty steel rails were purchased plus the necessary pointwork, thus allowing the alterations to commence on Monday 22nd August, 1899 after the last load of stone had passed over the turntable at 8 am. By 1 pm the following Friday the new siding, 80 ft long and passing under the gantry crane in Castletown yard, was in use.

In these days of the Welfare State with all its benefits - including sick pay for all - it is very easy to forget the way things were in those far off days at the turn of the century. When an employee became unfit and could no longer work, he had no income and had to live 'on the Parish' or reside in the Workhouse, only a lucky few finding places in 'Alms Houses'. Pensions were only obtainable (with a few exceptions) by former members of the Armed Forces, the Police, certain Government departments and for railway employees. The Portland company was a railway, but not in the same sense as the 264 large companies which were listed in the 1898 edition of *Bradshaw's Manual and Shareholders Guide*, in which it received no mention. No large amounts of capital were invested, as was the case with the bigger companies, and it was not therefore possible to pay pensions out of the interest or to absorb the cost out of the general finances of the business. The Portland company had generally been generous to their former employees when one takes into account their 'shoe string' finances, which relied entirely upon the revenue from one particular type of traffic. However, in January 1896 it was announced that the practice of paying full wages to sick employees would have to cease. Any employee not at work through disability would receive half pay for two weeks, after which all payment would stop. This action was a direct result of a poor trading year during 1895, for in that year only 32,346 tons of stone were carried over the railway - the lowest figure recorded since 1859.

For all the harsh new rules concerning gratuities a certain amount of compassion still prevailed. In April 1896 an old servant of the company, William Mears, became unfit to work, and the Directors granted a donation of £10 8s. to be paid to him within the year. Although at this time the Directors were at pains to emphasize that pensions and donations were no longer policy, a meeting in July 1896 not only granted Mears a pension of 4s. a week, but awarded Mr B. Hopkins, the Secretary, a gratuity of £21 for 'extra services rendered'.

During January 1899 the contract for shipping, moving, and loading the stone at Castletown, awarded to Joseph Hodder under an agreement dated 1875, was transferred to his son Abraham, who contracted to carry out the same work as his father for 2d. per ton and to supply a horse for the work for a fee of £1 5s. per week.

The 19th century was drawing to a close, and it is interesting at this point to reflect on the past 72 years of the company's operations - bearing in mind that several factors influencing its business were beyond its control. The amount of stone required by the building industry was subject to fluctuations then as it is today, and dependent on the economic conditions prevailing at the time. As an example of trade, we find that between January 1880 and December 1889, 890,888 tons of stone left the Island by way of the 'Merchants' Railway', earning the company £35,091 18s. 9d. The highest figure was 63,315 tons during 1899,

Loaded waggons wait at Castletown Pier. The simple 'stub points' used on this railway are shown in the foreground. *E. Latcham Collection*

A pre-World War I view of the west side of Castletown pier, showing the new steamer landing facilities of 1897; the shelter in the foreground was used by Naval personnel going to and from ships at anchor by liberty boat. Crowds flock ashore from the paddle steamer *Premier*, whilst in the background the coal hulks lie at anchor. To the right of the photograph waggons of stone await shipment from the east side of the pier. Note the young ladies spending their pennies on the amusement machines at about the last place one would expect to find some! As for the *Premier*, she was built on the Clyde in 1846 and commenced to operate between Weymouth and Portland in 1852, a service she continued until broken up in 1938, at which time she was the oldest steam vessel on Lloyds register. *Author's Collection*

A general view of Castletown pier taken after the Great War. A steam coaster is being loaded at the end of the pier and waggons await unloading. In the background are warships, coal hulks, and tugs, a bygone scene in a once busy harbour. *Author's Collection*

Stone being transferred from the waggons into a steam coaster at Castletown pier.
E. Latcham Collection

An aerial view of the Castletown area shortly after the end of World War II. 1) The Naval Hospital and adjacent buildings. 2) The Hospital Railway Halt. 3) Castletown exchange sidings. 4) Portland Castle. 5) The site of the stone loading jetties pre-1897. 6) The 'Merchants' Railway' incline.

E. Latcham Collection

and the lowest figure 32,346 tons during 1895 - the latter earning the company £1,321 8s. 6d. Although 1895 produced the lowest tonnage during the period, 1894 produced only one ton more, the declared figure being 32,347, but the earnings were substantially higher at £1,442 13s. 0d.

Although the Easton & Church Hope Railway had not yet opened, the 'Merchants' Railway' did not have the complete monopoly of stone traffic from the top of the Island, though one might have thought this to be the case. In 1888 it was estimated that between 5,000 and 6,000 tons of stone annually was transported by road through Fortuneswell. When the traction engine was introduced to Portland in the early 1890s it soon proved to be a very strong, powerful and flexible means of haulage, becoming yet another contestant in the stone transportation race.

One of the principal stone sawing mills was situated alongside the Weymouth & Portland Railway Company's station in Victoria Square, and rail access was provided to this mill, but the rates charged by the joint Great Western and London & South Western companies to convey stone from Castletown yard to the mill were high and discouraged quarry owners from using the service.

Throughout the years the biggest problem encountered by the Portland Railway was wear and tear on the machinery of the incline. As already mentioned, the use of chains to raise and lower the waggons had been superseded by wire ropes, the overhead drums also being replaced, and the following will give the reader an idea how long these ropes lasted and the tonnage each carried, together with the cost of replacement. One can clearly see that as wire rope became easier to manufacture and found a wider use in general industry it became less expensive.

A length of wire rope put into use during 1871 at a cost of £91 16s. 3d. lasted four years, during which time it lowered 213,803 tons of stone. Its replacement cost £87 18s. 9d. and lowered 364,803 tons in a life of 6½ years. It was again changed for wire of 3⅛th inch circumference, the 660 yards required costing £79 14s. 0d. This lowered 232,393 tons before needing to be replaced in 1887. In 1892 a wire rope of 3⅜th inch circumference was ordered at a cost of £59 9s. 0d. and this remained in service until 1901. Although the larger rope gave excellent service it was found to be a little too big for the job, so when it eventually wore out replacements of a smaller circumference were again taken into use.

As explained previously, the loaded waggons descended the incline counterbalanced by empty waggons ascending, the only method of control being by means of the brake drum which, when continually used, put a great strain on the wire rope, to say nothing of the wear on the brake drum itself. The system used since the introduction of wire rope consisted of a horizontal pulley with a brake wheel mounted above it which carried the rope while the top wheel acted as the brake drum. In 1885 Messrs Fowlers of Leeds fitted a new type of brake gear which consisted of a band of material around the brake drum which, when tightened, caused enough friction to bring waggons on the incline gradually to a halt. The system worked efficiently, but of course like most things was not without faults. It could stop the pulley turning but it did not trap the wire rope, and it was found that the rope would slip around its pulley

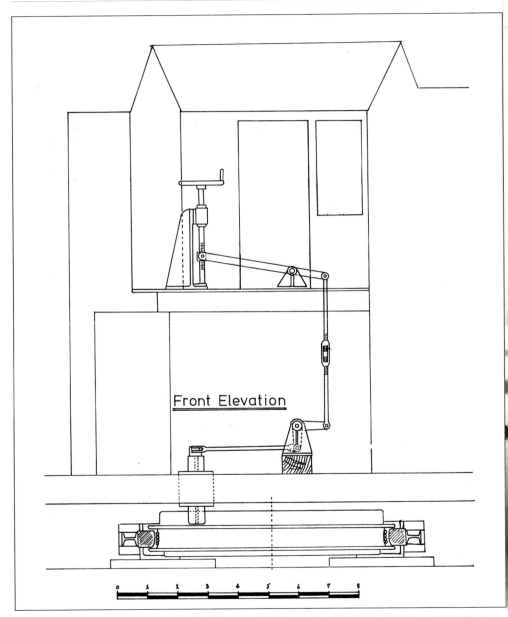

General arrangement drawings of replacement brake gear for the Portland Railway 1904, front elevation.

after the brake had been fully applied. There was also a tremendous strain on the actual brake drum - so much so that in March 1901 the brake wheel fractured resulting in damage to two waggons, and 20 roller pedestals had to be replaced.

In 1902 alterations were put in hand on the braking system to give the brakeman greater control, but whatever was done there remained tremendous torque on the brake wheel, a point demonstrated in September 1902 when the 2½ in. diameter shaft which operated the brake gear twisted, and had to be replaced by one of 3 in. diameter. The work was carried out by Messrs Bakers, a local engineering company.

By now parts of the braking mechanism were over 40 years old, and with continuous use great stress and strain had been put upon them. The company had to consider completely replacing the equipment. It was found that a new brakedrum of the overhead type would cost over £400, and taking into account various alterations that would be needed, the total cost would be around £600. Before making a final decision on further action, the Directors visited several similar inclines in Wales and Somerset in order to assess the type of gear other firms were using. It was finally decided to retain the existing system of a horizontal wheel and brake mounted on a vertical shaft housed at the side of the line at the top of the incline, but to modernise it.

A tender for the work from Messrs Stotherd & Pitt of Bath was accepted. The contract involved the fitting of a plain 8 ft diameter wire rope pulley wheel, and also an improved braking system which would grip the outer edge of the pulley wheel using wooden brake blocks, the blocks also pressing the wire into the groove to stop the old problem of wire slip during braking. The work on alterations to the brake drum started on 2nd January, 1905 and was completed 8½ days later.

Staff changes at management level had taken place over the past few years. On 30th June, 1900 Ben Hopkins resigned after 28 years as Company Secretary, and was replaced by Thomas Franklin Turner, who arrived in time to deal with a dispute regarding the semaphore signal on the incline. It will be recalled that since this signal was installed in 1876, the joint companies operating both the Weymouth & Portland Railway and the Admiralty railway to the Dockyard had paid the wages of the signalman. However in 1901 this payment ceased, and it had fallen upon the Portland company to pay the man's wages. Many letters passed between the companies involved in the dispute without any satisfactory solution being forthcoming, until finally Major-General Hutchinson of the Board of Trade was called in to arbitrate. The Major-General came to a decision in favour of the Portland Railway Company's claim that, on the basis of the existing agreement, the joint companies (GWR and LSWR) should be paying the signalman's wages. The joint companies appealed to the Queen's Bench Division of the High Court, but this appeal was dismissed and the joint companies had to pay the costs.

On 14th November, 1904, an agreement was signed between the Admiralty, GWR and LSWR concerning the replacement of the signal. The GWR, being responsible for the signalling of the Portland branch, agreed to install a bell and telephone system of communication between the brake drum on the

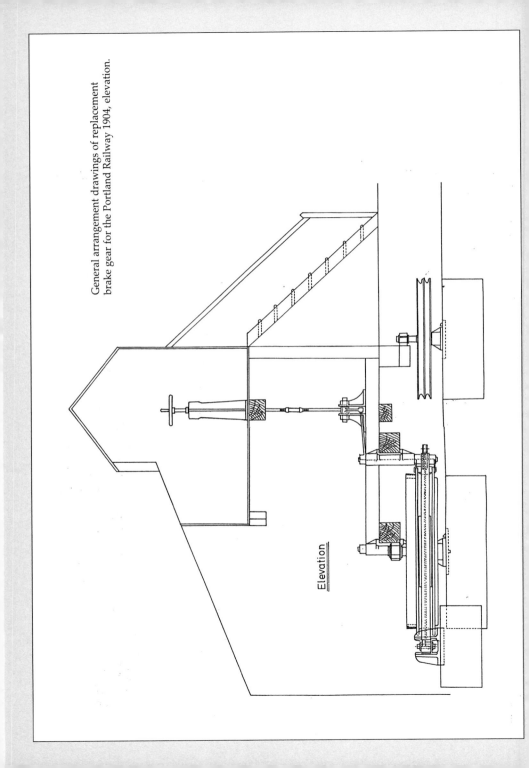

General arrangement drawings of replacement brake gear for the Portland Railway 1904, elevation.

Elevation

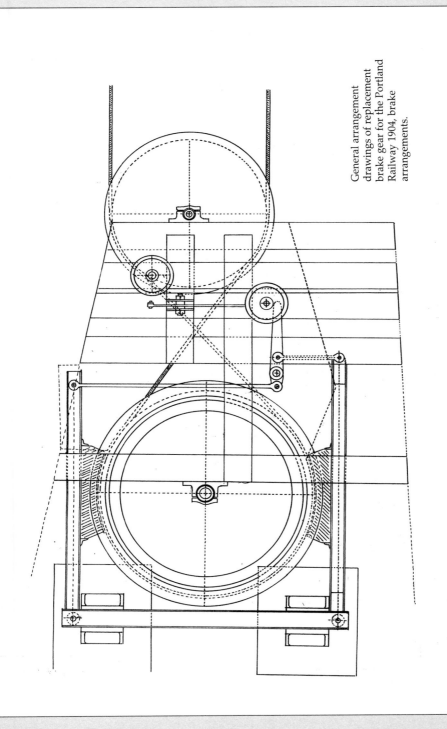

General arrangement drawings of replacement brake gear for the Portland Railway 1904, brake arrangements.

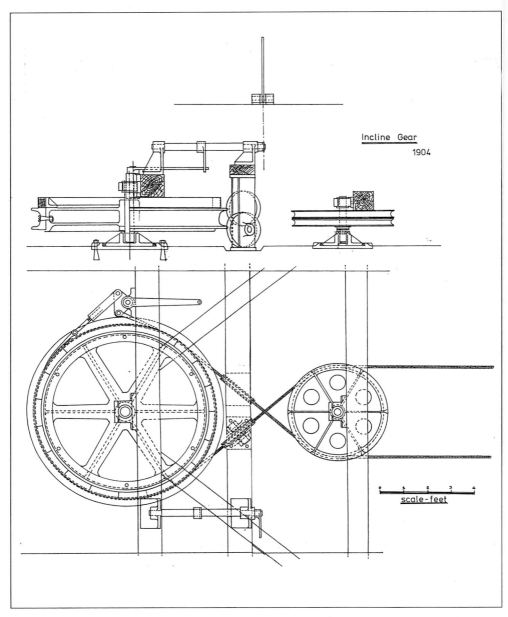

Incline Gear

1904

scale-feet

General arrangement drawings of replacement brake gear for the Portland Railway 1904, brake arrangements, end elevation and plan.

'Merchants' Railway' and the bottom of the incline at a cost not to exceed £40. All costs reasonably incurred in the maintenance of the system, provided they were certified by the Chief Accountant of the GWR, were to be repaid to the joint companies by the Admiralty on demand.

At a Directors' meeting held on 16th January, 1912, Henry John Sansom was elected Company Secretary following the death of Mr T.F. Turner. The outbreak of war on 4th August, 1914 marked a change in the way of life for everyone in industry, and the Portland Railway Company was no exception. Between January 1900 and December 1914, 842,152 tons of stone had been carried over the line,

In 1914 the SS *Malachite* sailed from Castletown pier with 530 tons of stone, one of the largest consignments ever shipped in one vessel, and the last ship to call before the war. The following slump in the building trade with very little work being carried out drastically reduced traffic over the line. During 1915 only 40,459 tons passed over the railway, and this fell to only 14,052 tons the following year.

Traffic continued to decline, and on 17th June, 1917 the railway ceased to operate. In the six months up to that date 2,065 tons had been carried, and at the half-yearly meeting held in July it was announced that the bank account held only £185 5s. 7d. in reserve. It was resolved to suspend all working of the railway until the Secretary could see some possibility of re-opening the line on a profitable basis. In January 1918 the Secretary took a 50 per cent cut in his salary, and by July 1919 the company's finances stood at exactly £120.

Once the war was over the building trade again started to flourish, and the Directors decided that Lloyds Bank be approached for a loan of £500, to be drawn on as required, to enable the line to resume operations. On 12th January, 1920 the line reopened for traffic,

During the war the rails of the incline to New Ground and several other feeder branches were removed, leaving only the main line from Priory Corner to the main incline and down into Castletown. The connecting lines of the various quarry owners had also been removed, and although not the direct property of the Portland Railway Company, they had still formed part of the system.

With the re-opening, a new scale of charges was introduced. Block stone from Priory Corner to Castletown now cost 1s. 7d. per ton, and another 4d. was charged as a loading fee at Castletown, whilst roach was to be carried at 1s. 2d. per ton. At the half-yearly meeting held in July a profit of £213 10s. 3d. was declared and a dividend of 5 per cent paid for the first half of the year. The price for conveying stone was again increased to 1s. 10d. a ton, and the conveyance of roach to 1s. 5d. - plus of course a handling charge.

William Mellish, the superintendent of the company, retired on 30th June, 1921 after 44 years of service, and was given a retirement bonus of £25 as a mark of appreciation for his services. His position was taken by Henry Attwooll.

At a company meeting in January 1922 a dividend of 7½ per cent was declared on the previous half-year's trading, a profit of £499 12s. 4d. having been also announced at this meeting. It was also decided to pay the Secretary the sum of £60 to compensate for his loss of salary during the war years.

An accident which occurred on 25th November, 1925 could have had more serious consequences than it did, when the wire rope snapped during the descent of several loaded waggons causing them to run free. Fortunately, the waggons turned over just before the 'swell'* and very little damage was done to the line, a similar accident taking place during April 1932.

In July 1926 the Directors decided to mark the company's centenary by giving each employee a bonus equivalent to one week's pay on 5th October. A look at the amount of traffic carried over the line during its 100 years of existence gives a good idea of the importance of the quarrying trade on the Isle of Portland. Between October 1826 and the end of September 1926 a total of 4,108,565 tons of stone had been transported. In the first three months of trading between October and December 1826, 4,803 tons travelled over the line, earning the company £289 2s. 1½d. For the corresponding period of 1926, 11,061 tons was carried to generate an income of £1,060 0s. 3d.

During a severe thunderstorm in the early hours of 24th March, 1927 lightning struck the crane at Priory Corner, damaging it beyond repair. A replacement was soon found and erected on the site. Henry Attwooll, superintendent of the line, retired in July 1928, the Directors deciding not to replace him.

There had been a steady revival of trade since the end of the Great War, the highest tonnage being 58,595 in 1930, and the lowest (up until 1939) 20,306 during 1933. The later figure brought about an operating loss of £147 16s. 8d. for the first half of that year. The General Strike and a depression in the building trade both had an affect on the stone industry, which in turn was reflected in the traffic returns of the 'Merchants' Railway', and indeed of the main line companies.

The arrival of the Easton & Church Hope Railway in 1900 also had an affect on the Portland Railway Company, but not to the extent that might have been expected. The introduction of legislation limiting the use of traction engines on public roads did little to help the company, and the arrival of the heavy diesel lorry in the 1930s soon made a drastic impact. But despite these new forms of transport, the Portland Railway - with its direct communication to the piers at Castletown - remained the best method of transportation for much of the stone and as late as April 1937 the SS *Test* loaded 400 tons for Liverpool.

During 1939, in the months leading up to the declaration of war on 3rd September, the stone trade rapidly decreased, although the company's half-yearly report showed a profit of £121 0s. 10d. resulting in a dividend of 7½ per cent being declared. There was, however, a definite turn for the worse in the three months ending 30th September, the total tonnage recorded being only 4,196 bringing in £402 0s. 11½d. With the outbreak of war almost all quarrying stopped, and this resulted in the line being closed on 11th October, 1939. During the last 11 days of trading it had carried only 315 tons for £33 12s. 9d.

Although it was not realised at the time, this was the end of the Portland Railway Company as an operating concern. Its life of service to the quarry owners of Portland had come to an end, but it had been of great benefit over the years, and had survived into a mechanical age. Such longevity was almost certainly brought about by its cheapness of operation, and its usefulness can be measured by the fact that during its working life it is estimated it carried a total of 4,561,796 tons of stone.

The closure of the line was naturally a severe blow to the company, no dividend being paid for the last half-year of 1939, whilst the Secretary took a 50 per cent cut

* Passing point.

in his salary to £40 per year. Following an application to the local Council, the rates payable on the railway were reduced to £10 per year for the duration of the war, and likewise rates on Crown lands at Castletown were reduced to £5 per year.

During 1940 the Military authorities applied to utilise certain buildings at the brake drum for the purpose of keeping pigs, but the Directors decided that this should not be allowed.

In June 1940 the Council tarred over the rails where they crossed the road at Castletown, and the line generally fell into decay. Early in 1944 the north face of the pier was converted into a slipway for the use of landing craft in connection with the impending invasion of Europe.

After the cessation of hostilities in 1945 there was little heart left to restart operations, for the motor lorry was now firmly established and a serious threat to goods business on the main line railways. On 11th February, 1945 Mr H.J. Sansom died, his place as Secretary being taken by Walter J. Sansom. Two years later the Chairman died, and was succeeded by Mr J. Croad.

The company now had very little income, but they were still faced with expenses and liabilities. To escape these a meeting of shareholders on 29th October, 1953 voted unanimously in favour of winding up the undertaking, and it was decided to apply to the Minister of Transport for a Warrant of Abandonment. To raise capital to continue until such time as a warrant was granted, £150 of 3½ per cent War Loans were sold to defray expenses.

At a meeting in July 1956 Mr W.F. Davis replaced Walter Sansom as Secretary, and also at this time it was decided to obtain tenders for the removal of the rails for scrap. The company had previously tried to obtain compensation for the rails that had been removed by the Admiralty at Castletown pier, but the Admiralty refused on the grounds that unless they were replaced and put into use again there could be no loss of value.

The condition of the building housing the brake wheel at the top of the incline was causing concern and it was pulled down in 1956, while at the same time tenders for the removal of the rails had been received. E.J. Farr & Company offered £152, J.H. Miller offered £407 17s. 6d., and W.L. Tait £720, but it was the tender of £760 sent in by Mr A. Scource that was accepted. Many of the rails still remain on the Island, for they were used as reinforcing in the new sea wall erected at Chiswell.

By this time the lease on the Crown lands had been surrendered, and the Ministry of Transport had decided that the Abandonment of Railways Act did not apply to the Portland Railway Company. Although the company was formed by an Act of Parliament, a clause in the original Act recited that when the Directors became less than five in number the company would be wound up, and this was now the case. Much of the company land was sold off at the best possible price. The final business matters of the company took place in 1972, after which the Portland Railway Company ceased to exist. Today building has taken place on parts of the former line. The remainder has been unaltered by the passage of time, and scars in the north face of the Island still show the route of the incline, but at its base a vast new Navy accommodation complex has been constructed completely obliterating the site and the former Castletown sidings. It is ironic that during the late 1950s when the Portland Railway Company was winding up its affairs, a new outlet was discovered for the spoils that had previously been tipped over the cliff edge. At Castletown pier

PORTLAND RAILWAY COMPANY.

Daily Summary of Loads run over the Incline during the month of

May 1937.

For **THE BATH & PORTLAND STONE FIRMS, LTD.**   **F. J. BARNES, LTD.**

Date	Loads	Tons	Ft.	In.	Date	Loads	Tons	Ft.	In.
3	12	93	9	.	3	6	47	.	.
4	16	121	10	.	4	10	76	4	.
5	16	123	10	.	5	9	68	13	.
6	9	69	5	.	6	12	86	13	.
7	19	143	4	.	7	1	7	11	.
8									
10	16	121	1	.	10	8	61	9	.
11	3	26	11	.	11	13	98	3	.
12									
13	18	138	4	.	13	2	14	2	.
14	8	61	12	.	14	28	219	10	.
15					15	2	15	5	.
17									
18									
19	18	142	2	.	19	4	30	13	.
20	17	132	1	.	20	10	76	1	.
21	22	165	13	.	21	10	78	7	.
22	3	22	14	.	22	4	30	13	.
24	8	60	12	.	24	11	86	15	.
25	9	70	1	.	25	21	162	12	.
26	7	7	7	.	26	8	64	8	.
27	4	31	4	.	27	20	156	1	.
28	5	39	.	.	28	22	171	7	.
29	3	24	7	.	29	4	31	4	.
31	14	110	6	.	31	4	30	13	.
Total	221	1705	5	.		209	1615	4	.

Sherren 280977

Load sheet May 1937.

a conveyor system was set up so that this stone - once thought to be rubbish - was brought to the pier in a fleet of lorries, loaded into ships, and transported away for use as flux in blast furnaces. However, this trade too has now declined, and very little stone is now shipped out. A small amount of fertilizer is now handled, but otherwise Castletown pier remains forlorn, a monument to the stone industry's great past.

Tonnage of Stone Carried over the 'Merchants' Railway'

The exact tonnage carried over the 'Merchants' Railway' cannot be stated. As no weighing facilities were ever installed, the method of achieving the load of each wagon, was by measuring the blocks of stone, and calculating the weight of the stone, 14 cubic feet = 1 ton. (1 cubic metre = 2.5 tons)

Human nature being what it is, there were certainly cases where figures were rounded up or down, a good guess taken, and the odd block or truck completely missed, all these discrepancies over the years mounting up!

However without the benefit of an exact science, the official loading records of the company are very detailed and give a good indication of both the state of the company and the industry. The peak year would appear to be 1904 with 93,133 tons carried, (despite the recent opening of the Easton & Church Hope Railway). In the first 91 years, 1826-1917, 3,860,720 tons travelled down the incline.

Re-opening after the Great War saw, with the odd exception tonnage in decline, 701,076 tons being carried during the 1920-1939 period. In the first three months of the line's opening, October-December 1826, 4,803 tons was carried, for the same period of the Centenary year, 11,061 tons was carried. But by that time the Portland Railway was an anachronism, although still able to compete with other forms of transport because of its simplicity!

Year	Tonnage	£	s.	d.	Year	Tonnage	£	s.	d.	Year	Tonnage	£	s.	d.
1880	48,912	2,140	8	5	1903	84,057	3,455	2	1	1932	32,641			
1881	55,387	1,903	14	10	1904	93,133	3,836	15	0	1933	20,306			
1882	45,967	1,714	9	0	1905	75,935	3,150	13	4	1934	26,902			
1883	46,187	1,729	7	1	1906	64,831	2,782	12	7	1935	31,641			
1884	36,474	1,507	3	8	1907	48,853				1936	28,585			
1885	43,082	1,707	19	3	1908	36,669				1937	31,842			
1886	40,432	1,624	14	0	1909	44,274				1938	33,014			
1887	37,035	1,492	7	2	1910	38,673				1939*	16,573			
1888	40,350	1,660	1	8										
1889	38,222	1,558	5	3	1915	40,459								
1890	38,850	1,552	5	10	1916	14,052								
1891	44,556	1,827	6	7	1917	2,065								
1892	42,323	1,762	1	5										
1893	44,680	1,856	0	4	1921	21,043	2,322	15	3					
1894	35,347	1,442	13	0	1922	29,588	3,016	5	2					
1895	32,346	1,321	8	6	1923	33,520	3,202	14	1					
1896	41,051	1,642	6	6	1924	21,151								
1897	55,098	2,091	19	8										
1898	61,674	2,429	17	11	1927	38,003								
1899	63,315	2,718	8	8	1928	35,626								
1900	49,285	2,106	14	7	1929	43,051								
1901	56,709	2,432	3	9	1930	58,595								
1902	71,161	3,026	6	1	1931	51,649								

	Tonnage
1825-1852	694,343
1853-1879	1,376,761
1880-1899	890,888
1900-1914	842,152
1915-1917	56,576
1825-1917	3,860,720
1920-1939	701,076
1825-1939	4,561,796

* Last week of operation 1st-11th October, 1939, 351 tons, £33 12s. 9d.

The timber staging used in the breakwater construction, viewed from the inner end of the outer breakwater arm. The line to the extreme left leads to the temporary bridge spanning the gap between the breakwater heads, just above can be seen the sloping earthworks of the first stage of the incline railway leading up to the Admiralty quarries. The track to the right leads to the site of the outer breakwater head, in the background are the gantries and other equipment at the base of the incline, with the 500 ft high Verne Hill towering behind.

William Thompson, courtesy John Thompson

The head of the inner breakwater viewed from the inner head of the outer breakwater, to the left the temporary timber bridge spanning the gap during the breakwater's construction.

William Thompson, courtesy John Thompson

Chapter Three

The Breakwater and Dockyard Railways

The Breakwater

The history of the Dockyard railways can be divided into two parts; firstly the construction of the original breakwater and the railways required to carry out this work, and secondly the branch line built from the Weymouth & Portland Railway to the Dockyard and its subsequent history.

It is difficult to imagine Portland before the days of the breakwater, Weymouth Bay providing only limited shelter in bad weather if the wind was blowing from a westerly direction, and the west side of Chesil Beach providing a lee if the wind blew from the east. This part of the Channel was a dangerous stretch of water as, apart from the limited protection provided by the Isle of Portland, there was no place of any size for a ship to shelter between the Isle of Wight and Plymouth. The story of shipping lost along this section of coast would fill several volumes.

John Harvey, clock maker to King George III and later Postmaster at Weymouth, knew that the French had constructed a massive fortified breakwater at Cherbourg, 60 miles across the Channel. In 1794 Harvey suggested plans for a breakwater at Portland to provide a naval base and a safe anchorage for ships in bad weather. Whilst the proposals were being discussed, vessels of Admiral Christian's fleet foundered on Chesil Beach during November 1795 on passage to the West Indies. Despite this and other disasters, little interest was shown in the scheme until the 1820s, when Harvey's son (also John) revived the project. A Bill was drawn up to go before Parliament 'For constructing a breakwater in Portland Roads', but again little support was forthcoming and the matter proceeded no further.

In October 1835 a meeting was called in Portland to give further consideration to the matter, as it was becoming clear that some form of breakwater would have to be constructed in the near future. At this meeting a committee was formed to protect the rights of the Islanders if such work went ahead. But nothing more happened until 1844, when a Naval Commission tasked with the selection of suitable places for harbours of refuge stated that Portland, being halfway between Portsmouth and Plymouth, was well suited, and the materials for the breakwater's construction were readily available. Further surveys were carried out in late 1846, and to enable work on the project to commence an Act of Parliament was passed on 11th May, 1847. The Act empowered 'The Commissioners of Her Majesty's Woods' to purchase land for the purpose of building a breakwater and harbour of refuge. Compensation of £20,000 was paid to the Portlanders for the loss of lands and rights, including common land on The Verne required for a fort and, not unlike similar compensation cases in later years, extra legislation was introduced to stop disagreement on how the money was to be divided up.

Up to that time the only military installations in the area were the castles at Portland and Sandsfoot, built in the reign of Henry VIII, that at Sandsfoot being

An early engraving with much artist's licence, showing the pier heads of the South Ship Channel. On the landward section of the breakwater is a locomotive, in the distance behind the outer pierhead an impression of the construction staging.

View from head of outer breakwater looking towards Portland, the head of the inner breakwater is across the South Ship Channel. To the left is the temporary bridgework across the gap, in the foreground the wooden staging and broad gauge rails used during construction, in the background the buildings of the future dockyard.   *Weymouth & Portland Museum Services*

a ruin, and several Cavalry Barracks constructed in the Weymouth area during the Georgian period. These were for the accommodation of troops protecting King George III during his frequent visits to the town.

The Napoleonic invasion fears of the 18th century, although followed by the victories at Trafalgar and Waterloo, did little to remove apprehensions in the 19th century, particularly when the French constructed forts at Cherbourg and there was a general introduction of more sophisticated weaponry including ironclad warships.

The work, which was originally intended to be simply a breakwater, quickly developed into a massive defence system to protect the Weymouth and Portland area. The projects involved were a fort on the north side of Portland (on top of Verne Hill) protected by a dry moat, gun emplacement at East Weares, a fort on the end of the breakwater (later known as Chequers Fort), the Nothe Fort at the entrance to Weymouth Harbour, and Upton Fort at Osmington Mills on the east side of Weymouth Bay. As guns were rapidly improving at this time and the cannon ball had become a thing of the past, the position of these new fortifications gave cover to the whole of Weymouth Bay with the artillery then available.

Notwithstanding that the Act of Parliament was not yet passed (!), preliminary work commenced at once. In August 1848 construction was started of the gravity-operated railway from the Grove down the east side of the Verne to the north-east corner of the island situated 400 ft below, from which point the breakwater was to commence. Peter Thompson, a London contractor, was engaged in the construction of the temporary prison to house the convicts who were shortly to arrive and form a valuable workforce on the project. The first of these arrived at Portland on 20th November, 1848 when the *Driver* landed 64 convicts at Castletown, to be joined by 236 more shortly afterwards.

One of the first tasks given to these prisoners was the construction of a road from the prison to Easton (now known as Grove Road). Meanwhile work had progressed well on the incline railway, the ropes having been fitted to the brake drums in June.

The following year contractors started quarrying stone from what was to form the Verne Ditch for the breakwater, the material being lowered down a rope-operated incline from the east side of the Verne to join up with the incline running down from the Grove. In that June the convicts opened a quarry for their own use and to supply stone for the breakwater, it being reported that:

> . . . 119 convicts on average per day, [are] working on forming embankments and excavations for railway lines to the incline railway, laying the sleepers, track and ballasting the same, levelling ground for sheds, getting out and stacking stone, filling into wagons and drawing to and from the incline railway for the Breakwater.

It was part of a revolutionary scheme for prisoners sentenced to transportation to the Colonies. After sentencing they first went to a closed prison, then to a second stage at a prison engaged in public works, such as Portland, where they could be employed in quarrying and general construction work (but not working on the actual breakwater), which gave them a trade. Prisoners who were well behaved were then given a 'ticket of leave' which

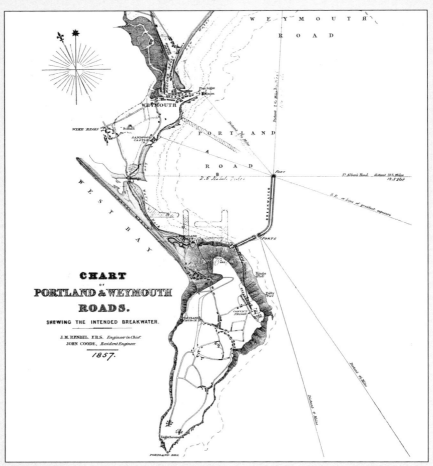

A chart drawn up by Messrs Rendell and Coode, showing the intended breakwater. Although dated 1857 various amendments have been overdrawn, including the proposed Weymouth & Portland Railway. Other various markings added include the site of the northern arm of the breakwater, and various additions in the Dockyard, Castletown and Mere area. The only railways shown are the Admiralty incline, and the basic 'Merchants' Railway'.

Section plan of original breakwater.

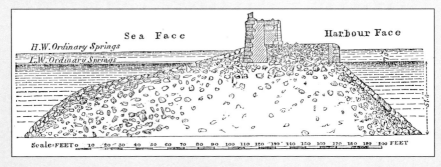

entitled them to wages and other privileges whilst serving the third part of their sentence in the Colonies, a system that was discontinued in 1868.

The Foundation Stone of the breakwater was dropped onto the sea bed by Prince Albert, the Prince Consort, on 25th July, 1849. The Prince travelled from Osborne House, on the Isle of Wight, by boat to Southampton and thence by train to Dorchester, by carriage to Weymouth, and finally by boat to Portland, thus clearly demonstrating the difficulty of travel in those days. An account of his visit states that, following the sinking of the foundation stone, the Royal party travelled up the incline to the prison in three special wagons covered with crimson cloth!

Unfortunately very few details of the railway used in the execution of these works have survived, most of the information being in the form of eye witness accounts from people who visited the site. The incline itself, on a gradient varying from 1 in 10 to 1 in 15, consisted of three slopes, each 1,500 ft long, in line with each other. At the top of each slope there was an overhead brake drum 12 ft in diameter fitted with a powerful screw brake which controlled the cable for each section. Fully loaded descending wagons hauled the empty ones up on two separate 7 ft broad gauge railway tracks. At the top of the first incline there was a weighbridge, which not only weighed the wagons but also recorded the number passing over it each day so that an accurate record of the traffic could be maintained.

To enable the breakwater to be built substantial timber staging was erected on piles, some up to 120 ft long, having large iron 'Mitchell' screws at the base to enable them to dig into the clay of the sea bed to a depth of between six and eight feet. These piles and the other baulks of timber were bolted together and bound with iron bands to form a structure 123 ft wide capable of withstanding the wrath of the sea. Railway tracks were laid along the top of the staging, which had no decking, so that wagons holding some 10 tons of stone apiece could be propelled to the required position, where a pin was withdrawn to allow the stone to drop through a trap door in the floor of the wagon into the sea below. By making use of the five tracks which covered the full width of the staging, the profile of the breakwater was gradually built up. The staging, parts of which were buried within the work, was gradually extended at its outer end as work progressed.

A description of a visit made to the site by Charles Dickens in 1858 gives a good insight into the working of the railway.

Up the hill to the right run the inclines; the heavy four wagon trains rattle down them and flit by us, each with *Prince Albert* or *Prince Alfred* puffing away behind, and dashing them off rapidly to the far end of the cage. A good railed passage is provided leading between two of the five broad gauge roads which run to the end of the inner breakwater abreast over open rafters. Six hundred yards from the shore the inner breakwater ends in a noble bastion-like head, rising with smooth round sides, some 30 feet above the waves. A space of 400 feet separates this head from its partner, a precisely similar work, set on the end of the outer breakwater. The staging at this point is carried out a little to the right (not passing over the heads, but swerving slightly from them) and is narrowed to three lines of road instead of five; but, upon reaching the outer limb of the work, the five lines immediately re-assemble, and go on together all the rest of the way. The

A view of construction of the outer breakwater head, clearly showing the wooden staging and one of the broad gauge railway lines.   *Weymouth & Portland Museum Services*

An engraving of the Admiralty works at Portland first published in 1861. It clearly shows the viaduct across the opening between the breakwater heads, and other well known buildings have already become established on the site.

The Admiralty incline viewed from the top of East Weares during 1877, showing the middle brake drum. The road alongside the incline leads away to the right up the hill, where part of the original prison is just visible. *Royal Engineers Library, Chatham*

An enlargement of the previous photograph showing the middle brake drum of the Admiralty incline. To the left two loaded stone wagons appear to be descending, whilst three empty wagons are nearer the drum. *Royal Engineers Library, Chatham*

East Weare A and B gun batteries looking north-east photographed in December 1877. In the background lies the completed breakwater. In the right foreground the brake drum and trackwork of an incline that ran up the east side of the Verne. Little is known of this incline as it is not shown on any maps of the period. It would appear to form a junction with the main Admiralty incline which ran at right angles out of view to the right.

Royal Engineers Library, Chatham

Convicts at work constructing the walls of the Verne West Ditch during 1877. The primitive equipment, and lack of safety precautions would give a present day Health and Safety official apoplexy!   *Royal Engineers Library, Chatham*

intervening piece of three-line staging is the perfect part of the whole cage, its firm unyielding timbers will bear, almost without vibration, the 48 tons of the loaded wagons, and the weight of the engine too.

After describing much other detail of the breakwater, Dickens continues,

Every two or three minutes comes rumbling behind us a train with its four loaded wagons, each wagon averaging 12 tons in weight. An ordinary load consists of a large block in the centre, some two or three feet in diameter, around which are heaped fragments of smaller sizes, the whole rising to a considerable height in the wagon. It is a fine thing to watch the tipping of the rubble through the open rafters of the cage. Every wagon has a dropping floor, slant going downwards from back to front, but with its ironwork lighter and less massive in front than behind. It is so contrived that a brakesman, with a few blows of his hammer, knocks away the check, and sets the floor free to drop; the front drops at once, because, owing to its greater depth, it is pressed by the greater weight of stone. The whole mass tumbles with a confused uproar on to the rubble heap below, and then the heavy iron work behind causes the floor at once to return to its natural position, in which it is immediately re-fastened. A puff or two of the engine brings each wagon in succession over the required spot.

To construct the circular head of the Breakwater Fort, train loads of stone were brought to a steam-operated traveller that swung two or three wagons in a wide circle depositing material where it was required.

Building a breakwater to take the force of the sea and the weight of the fortifications involved a little more than just dumping stone into the sea, and for the construction of the fort at the far end of the breakwater (Chequers Fort) certain specified materials were to be used. A letter from John Coode, the engineer in charge, also gives an insight into the railway working:

No material to be loaded into wagons except the flint beds and clean rubble, clean quarry chippings, and grit, free from all admixture of earth and soil. The largest stones for this purpose must not exceed two tons, but when stones of this size are sent, they must not be more than one 'craned' or heavy stone in each wagon. When stones of one ton to one-half ton each are sent, they must not be more than two 'craned' or heavy stones in each wagon. The remainder of the load in each case to be made up with rubble, sprawls and chippings of all sizes, from stones of 2 cwt. each down to fine grit, mixed in such proportions as will make the mass compact and free from interstices. [The final part of the letter concludes,] The wagons containing this special foundation material must be sent to the weigh-bridge in separate trains and marked with a distinguishing plate.

Derailments and accidents were commonplace on this work, often causing death or injury. Twenty-two men died as a result of accidents during the construction work and five others were drowned. The first serious accident took place on 13th November, 1853 when, owing to part of the staging collapsing, a locomotive, four wagons and eight workmen fell into the sea. The driver and fireman of the engine jumped clear, but two workmen were drowned, crushed under the falling rocks. The locomotive and wagons were later recovered.

A convict was killed in September 1855 when he fell in front of a engine near the quarries. The job was certainly fraught with dangers, some of which were self-inflicted. Riding on wagons was not allowed, but George Milton was killed in May 1857 whilst taking a single loaded wagon down the incline without using the drum and brake system. During the descent he was unable to reach the wagon brake, and met his end by being thrown under the wagon when it crashed at the bottom. Two years later a labourer was killed following the derailment of a wagon in which he was riding on the staging.

Despite the fact the construction site was a dangerous place, visitors were encouraged to view the work in progress from a walkway that extended to the end of the staging. In September 1857 a lady was on the walkway when her dress caught in something and she was dragged under the wheel of a passing stone truck and killed!

In July 1859 the failure of a bolt on the brake gear of one of the drums caused a load to run out of control. As the loaded wagons gained speed on their descent, the ascending empties did likewise and shot past the drum, taking the unfortunate brakesman with them over a drop. Three months later a drum went out of control, killing a worker who was caught in the whirling equipment. A further fatality occurred when timber was being brought down the incline in a wagon, its speed being controlled by a sprag. A man slipped and died after his head struck one of the roller guides of the incline cable. In January 1860 a train load of stone fell into the sea from the temporary bridge spanning the southern entrance of the breakwater, and during the same year two locomotives collided on a section of railway running around the side of the Verne fortifications.

The untamed force of the sea also caused dislocation of the work. A severe storm in April 1858 carried away five sections of the pile structure, and the following year the viaduct spanning the south entrance was severely damaged when a 200 ft length was destroyed during a gale. The construction of the breakwater itself was to cause even more accidents. On Tuesday 14th February, 1860 the small schooner *Alert* of Pembroke became the first of many vessels to founder after running into the breakwater.

Work was progressing well and Prince Albert, who showed a great interest in the Portland project, made another visit. On Tuesday 8th August, 1861 the Royal Yacht arrived at Portland; on board was the Prince Consort, the Prince and Princess Frederick William of Prussia, Prince Arthur and their respective suites.

Following the usual formalities with various personages upon landing, the male members of the party proceeded up the incline to survey the fortifications on the East Weare and Verne Hill. They were shown over the entire works, the batteries, roads, covered ways, the ditch and excavation for magazines. The party then ascended the sides of the hill to reach the level of the railway that encircled Verne Hill.

Spectacular progress had been made at the Verne site, more so when one considers the equipment available to contractors at that period. By 1862 Messrs Jay & Company had completed its contract which had required it to dig the ditch (but not build up the walls), construct 50 arched accommodation casements, and excavate the main drainage system and water storage tanks. An amount of stone quarried in the Verne was used for its construction, the surplus being used elsewhere on the Island's Government works. The amount extracted in the ditch from the Chert beds below the building stone was approximately 1,824,545 tons. When the building stone extracted is added it comes to a total of approximately 2,794,266 tons.

Work continued on the Verne under a combination of both convict and contract labour, assisted and under the direction of the Royal Engineers, and although the completion date 1881 is displayed above the North Gate, work was still being carried out in 1889.

At the same time the Nothe Fort, across the water at the entrance to Weymouth Harbour, gave difficulties. Work had commenced in 1860, but two years later the contractor withdrew and it was completed in 1872 by the Royal Engineers, assisted with contract labour. The stone was transported by barge from Portland.

James Meadows Rendel designed the breakwater and was the Engineer in Chief until his death in 1856, when John Coode, who was Resident Engineer, took over his post. Much of the work was put out to contract, several parties being involved. One was Phillip Dodson who was also involved in various works at Weymouth, another John Towlerton Leather, who at that period was involved in several other Government contracts, and also owned the Hunslet Engine Company of Leeds.

The railway used in the construction work was of the broad gauge (7 ft), and initially horses were used to haul the wagons onto the staging, until the Summer of 1851 when the first steam locomotive commenced work, by which time 1,000 ft of infill had already been deposited. In August 1854 three new locomotives were delivered to the breakwater site.

Details of the engines used in this work are a little vague. Despite a large amount of research conducted by the Industrial Railway Record Society and others, not all the answers are forthcoming. Five 0-4-0 broad gauge well tanks, built by E.B. Wilson of Leeds in 1852, were used during the construction work. Of these No. 329 *Queen* is the best recorded, a surviving photograph of her (judging by the the staging and equipment around her) being taken at Portland. *Queen* was built with inside sandwich frames. The four 4 ft driving wheels had a wheelbase of 8 ft, whilst the two inside cylinders were 10½ in. bore with a 17 in. stroke. The water tank held 150 gallons, and the domeless boiler, with raised firebox, was pressurised at 120 psi. Following work on the breakwater, she was sold in 1868 to the Torbay & Brixham Railway for the opening of its two mile branch from Churston to Brixham. In 1879 the engine was mortgaged to the South Devon Railway and included in its stock from July that year. On 1st January, 1883 the Torbay & Brixham Railway was purchased by the Great Western Railway, *Queen* being added to Great Western stock and withdrawn the same day, but she spent some years in a siding at Swindon before being broken up.

From research it would appear that the other four engines were of the same class with only detail difference to distinguish them. By 1878, following completion of the works at Portland, these four engines had been acquired by I.W. Boulton of Ashton-under-Lyne, who owned an engineering company and was also a dealer in second-hand contractors' locomotives. In his book

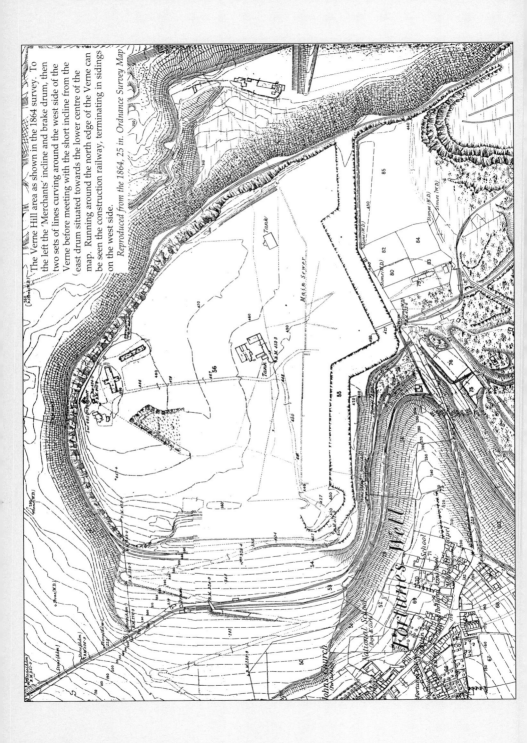

The Verne Hill area as shown in the 1864 survey. To the left the 'Merchants' incline and brake drum, then two sets of lines curving around the west side of the Verne before meeting with the short incline from the east drum situated towards the lower centre of the map. Running around the north edge of the Verne can be seen the construction railway, terminating in sidings on the west side.

Reproduced from the 1864, 25 in. Ordnance Survey Map

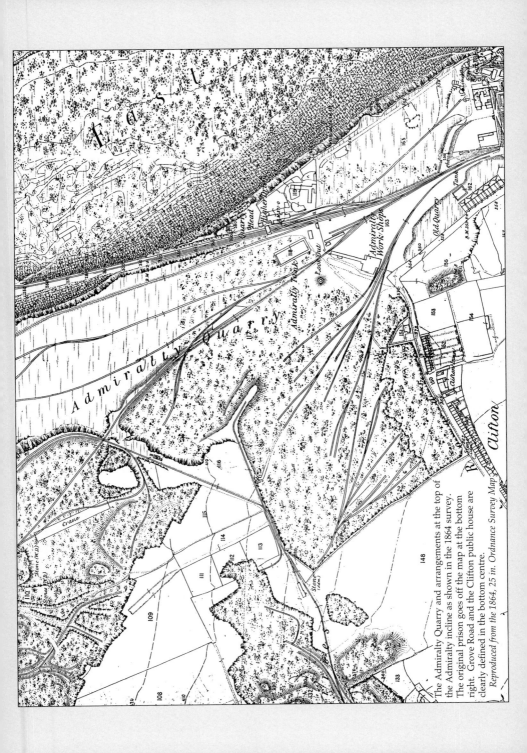

The Admiralty Quarry and arrangements at the top of the Admiralty incline as shown in the 1864 survey. The original prison goes off the map at the bottom right. Grove Road and the Clifton public house are clearly defined in the bottom centre.

Reproduced from the 1864, 25 in. Ordnance Survey Map.

The south-west casemates of the Verne Fort, looking west photographed during 1877. To the left in the foreground in front of the group of workmen a railway track used during construction work within the Verne Fort can be seen. The main parade ground was to the right of the picture. Since 1949 these fine buildings have formed part of HM Prison, Verne. Ironically it was convicts of a past generation that helped construct accommodation for future inmates.

Royal Engineers Library, Chatham

The east side of Verne Hill viewed from the air. The large group of buildings are the HMS Osprey complex. The principal points of interest are marked on the photograph as follows: A. Verne Ditch. B. High level construction railway. C. Admiralty incline Railway (1847). D. Easton & Church Hope Railway. E. East Weare Batteries. *HMS Osprey Photographic Section*

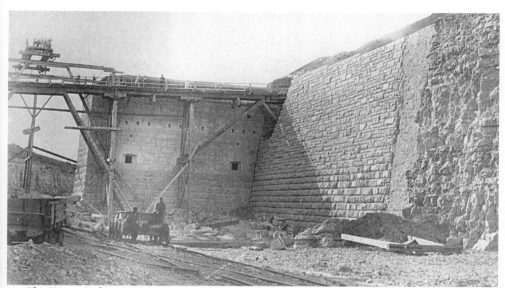

The Verne ditch in 1865, during construction of the South Gate. In this historic photograph looking west, two rail wagons are shown, and note the unusual type of pointwork in the foreground. The temporary timber bridge in the background also carried a railway, a gantry crane is also shown which allowed the transfer of materials between the railway in the ditch and the higher level of fort construction. *Royal Engineers Library, Chatham*

An engraving that first appeared in 1862, showing the Great Moat around the Verne under construction.

The south-west ditch of the Verne, looking east during 1877. The railway line along the base of the ditch curves away to the right towards the South Gate.

Royal Engineers Library, Chatham

The west ditch of the Verne photographed during 1877. The masonry walls have been erected, in the left corner can be seen a Sallyport and drawbridge protected by a small ditch. On the right there is a flight of removable stairs, and a railway line can be seen running along the ditch floor.
Royal Engineers Library, Chatham

Work on construction looking towards the South Gate of the Verne Fort. In the absence of photographs, engravings like this convey the magnitude of these great works.

Outline drawing of 0-4-0 broad gauge locomotive of the type supplied by E.B. Wilson and used
during the construction of the breakwater.   *M.J. Tattershall*

0-4-0 well tank *Queen*, built by E.B. Wilson of Leeds in 1852, one of four such locomotives used
during the construction of the original breakwater, photographed at Portland during this
period.   *Real Photographs*

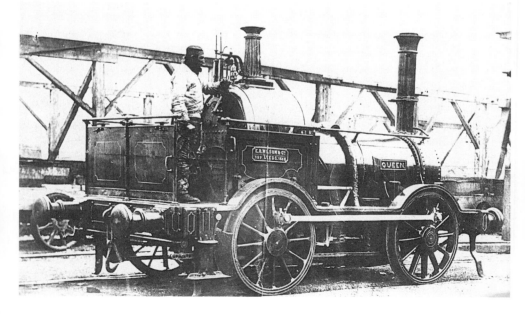

The Prince of Wales, laying a stone to commemorate the completion of the original breakwater in 1872.
Illustrated London News

The stone laid by the Prince of Wales on 10th August, 1872, to commemorate the completion of the original breakwater works.
W. Macey

FROM THIS SPOT
ON THE 25TH OF JULY 1849,
HIS ROYAL HIGHNESS PRINCE ALBERT
CONSORT OF QUEEN VICTORIA.
SUNK THE FIRST STONE OF THIS BREAKWATER.

UPON THE SAME SPOT,
ALBERT EDWARD. PRINCE OF WALES.
ON THE 10TH OF AUGUST 1872.
LAID THIS LAST STONE
AND DECLARED THE WORK COMPLETE.

THESE ARE IMPERIAL WORKS
AND WORTHY KINGS.

Inscription on the stone unveiled by the Prince of Wales on 10th August, 1872, to commemorate
the completion of the original breakwater works.   *W. Macey*

A view taken at Castletown during the construction of the Admiralty line between the
Weymouth & Portland Railway and the breakwater. The formation of the Verne Fort then under
construction can be seen at the top of the picture.   *Author's Collection*

Chronicles of Boulton's Sidings, Bennett mentions these engines, although their names and numbers were missing (except No. 454), and adds that by this time there was no market for broad gauge locomotives and they were converted to portable and winding engines. A.P. Bell of Manchester purchased one for £359, and one of the others went to the Denton Colliery Company.

Bennett also states that two standard gauge 0-6-0 tender engines were purchased from the Portland breakwater by Boulton, and when in his yard were named *Lord Warden* and *Lord Roberts*, but there is little to support this statement. Dickens gave account of engines named *Prince Albert* and *Prince Alfred*, but no other details.   As one of the engines was named *Queen* it would not be unreasonable to assume that two of the other four well tanks were the two 'Princes'!

The original breakwater, consisting of two arms, was completed on Saturday 4th March, 1871 when the last stone was laid in the presence of Mr Coode, the Engineer in Chief. It is estimated that nearly six million tons of stone went into its construction. At the peak between 2,500 and 3,000 tons a day were being delivered from the various quarries, the record being 25,000 tons in one week. On 10th August, 1872 the Prince of Wales (later King Edward VII) arrived at Portland aboard the Royal Yacht to declare the project complete. He unveiled a stone with the inscription,

> From this spot on 25th July, 1849, His Royal Highness Prince Albert, Consort to Queen Victoria, sank the first stone of this Breakwater. Upon the same spot, Albert Edward, Prince of Wales, on 10th August 1872 laid this last stone and declared the works complete. These are imperial works and worthy Kings.

The crowning glory of these works was the Breakwater (later Chequers) Fort at the end of the breakwater. It was 110 ft in diameter with walls made up of three thicknesses of 6½ in. plate faced with granite. The foundations up to high water mark had been supervised by Mr Coode, the actual fort being constructed by contractors under the supervision of the Royal Engineers. Completed in the mid-1870s, it was fully armed by 1880.

The Dockyard and the New Breakwaters

During the construction of the breakwater a rough line had been laid to connect with the 'Merchants' Railway' at Castletown, but there was no direct connection either with this or the Weymouth & Portland Railway. Therefore the next logical step was to construct a line into what was later to become the Dockyard. The first mention of this appeared in the *Dorset County Chronicle* on 15th September, 1870, where it stated; 'The works for the extension of the Weymouth & Portland Railway to the Breakwater will commence on October 1st'. This statement would appear to have been speculation, as no agreement was reached until the following year when, under Section 62 of the Great Western Railway (Additional Powers) Act of 1871, the construction of a railway, 1 mile 3.40 chains long, between the Admiralty breakwater and the Weymouth & Portland Railway, was authorised.

Map of the various tramways on the Island north of Easton *circa* 1870. Easton is at the bottom of the map, the Admiralty incline is seen on the right hand side, clearly showing the position of the three drums, the blank space in the bottom right, past the Admiralty workshops is the site of the prison. The extensive Admiralty quarries are clearly marked. The cluster of quarries in the centre of the map alongside Easton Lane (later the site of the Sawmill Tavern, and Steward's offices) also shows the tramway alongside Easton Lane, that curves away into Sheepcroft. The Verne, to the top right, is shown with the railway running around the outer edge, to the left the lines of the Portland Railway are shown around the edge of the Verne and along the northern flank of Yeates.

Reproduced from the 1864, 25 in.
Ordnance Survey Map

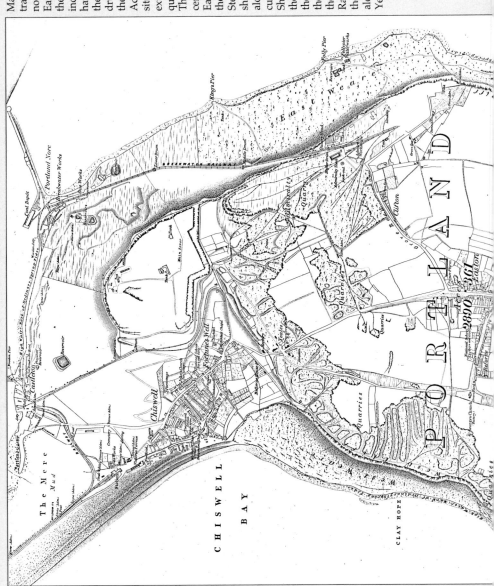

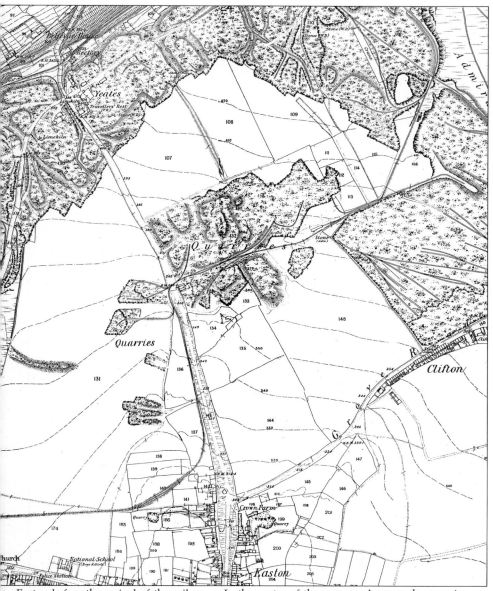

Easton before the arrival of the railway. In the centre of the map can be seen the quarries alongside Easton Lane, where the tramway crossed Easton Lane was the site of the Sawmill Tavern. The tramway then followed Easton Lane before turning to head out towards West Cliff. Just below where the tramway curved was later to be the site of Sheepcroft Yard on the Easton & Church Hope Railway. The quarries to the right of the map were part of the Admiralty workings.

Reproduced from the 1864, 25 in. Ordnance Survey Map

A general view of the dockyard facilities in the 1890s, the railway is shown fully signalled, the signal box tucked back against the bank where later the Easton line was to be built. The large raised building with the tipping facilities was a coal store, the building still surviving known as 'Monkey Island'; on the centre right the offices of the breakwater engineer, later used by the First Officer Sea Training.   *J.H. Lucking Collection*

A general view of the dockyard taken following the opening of the Easton & Church Hope Railway, which ran along the base of the hillside in the foreground.   *Author's Collection*

The Act was a very involved document set against a background of the great changes that had taken place over the preceding years. The original agreement was that the railway companies would construct, at their own expense, upon land either provided by the Admiralty or acquired by the railway companies, a single line of standard gauge railway, together with all necessary communications, turnouts, sidings, signals, turntables and other conveniences required for its working. The Admiralty were to pay the railway companies an annuity of £4 per cent on the cost of the construction of the line and the acquisition of the land required for the purpose. There appeared to be no hurry to carry out this work, but in July 1873 nearly all the inhabitants of Castletown received notice to quit their homes in order to make way for the proposed railway. It is noteworthy that the only buildings to be left standing were The Castle Inn and an adjoining cottage.

There is very little recorded about the construction of the line, mainly owing to the fact it was not a public railway, but also because the work was of a very minor nature compared with the other great works that were being carried out in the area.

Eleven tenders were received for the construction of the line, the contract being awarded to Messrs Robinson & Adams, and work commenced on 28th July, 1874. There is little doubt that work on the project had not commenced earlier owing to the imminent removal of the broad gauge from the Wilts, Somerset & Weymouth section of the GWR and the Portland branch in the June of that year. Much of the broad gauge line on the breakwater works was relaid as standard gauge, and where possible the existing rails were re-used. According to GWR records construction was completed in February 1876, and the *Southern Times* for 15th July of the same year reported, 'Although the new line between the terminus at Portland and the Breakwater is completed, no public opening has yet taken place'. A week later the same paper reported that 'A Great Western train passed over the line on Wednesday. A few alterations must be made in laying the metals before the railway can be declared open'. In March 1877 the local press declared that 'Landslips have caused delay in the opening of the railway line to the Breakwater', but in fact it was not until early 1878 that the line was open to traffic.

The Act of Parliament laid down very thorough details to protect the rights and workings of the Portland Railway Company. The bridge over that company's line at the bottom of the incline was subject to particular specifications, a clearance of not less than 11 ft being required. Furthermore, as we have seen, as the bridge would obstruct the view of the bottom of the incline from the top, a semaphore signal was to be provided to assist in the working of the incline.

It was ordered that the line be constructed with 75 lb. flat bottom track of the best quality, with creosoted sleepers of Baltic timber 9 ft long, 8 in. wide and 5 in. deep; the entire work to be carried out to a standard that would permit the Board of Trade to approve it for the working of passenger traffic. Under an agreement dated 29th May, 1874 the railway companies were to have management and control of the railway, and would also bear the expense of all signals and switches as well as providing the signalmen and switchmen required to operate the line. They were to charge 3*d*. per ton for all goods and merchandise carried over the railway. For passengers the charges were to be 3*d*. first class, 2*d*. second class and 1*d*. third class other than soldiers, officers, sailors and other Government employees.

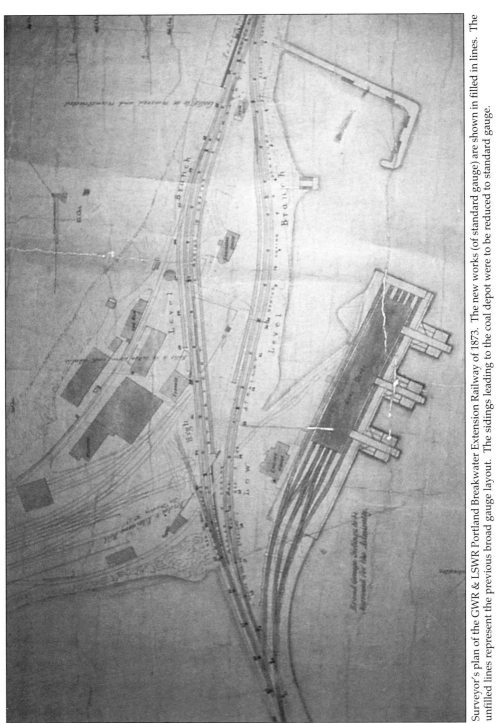

Surveyor's plan of the GWR & LSWR Portland Breakwater Extension Railway of 1873. The new works (of standard gauge) are shown in filled in lines. The unfilled lines represent the previous broad gauge layout. The sidings leading to the coal depot were to be reduced to standard gauge.

It was a rather unusual line inasmuch that the Board of Trade insisted on it being fully interlocked and signalled in case the need to convey troops should arise in an emergency. The only regular traffic, however, was freight hauled mainly by horses.

Details of the signalling equipment on the line have disappeared with the passage of time. However from surviving photographs it would appear that at least the signals were of the 'Stevens' Pattern, and mainly of the slotted post variety. The signal box at the Dockyard was known as Portland No. 2.

During the 1870s there was a demand for coaling facilities as steam merchant ships were fast replacing sail, and several companies set up business supplying coal from hulks moored in Portland Harbour. In October 1881 one merchant, Messrs G.H. Collins of Dartmouth, asked the Admiralty to use part of the breakwater for storing coal and bunkering merchant ships, or if this were not acceptable if the GWR could forward coal wagons to that point for trans-shipment into hulks. Various correspondence passed between the Director of Works for the Navy and both the GWR and LSWR companies, and by June 1882 a letter from the Great Western to the Director of Navy Works stated that it 'had no objection to permission being granted to Messrs Collins to have coal conveyed by rail over the Admiralty line, as our arrangement with the Admiralty provides for this'. Remaining records do not record the outcome, but it was generally the practice to refill the hulks from colliers, except for vessels of the Royal Navy, as the old sailing ships which the original breakwater had been designed to protect were replaced by the power of steam - a development which called for first class maintenance and servicing facilities.   Portland became a coaling station, and although the coal store on 'Monkey Island' was adequate at first, during 1889 provision was made in the Naval Estimates for expanded coaling arrangements.

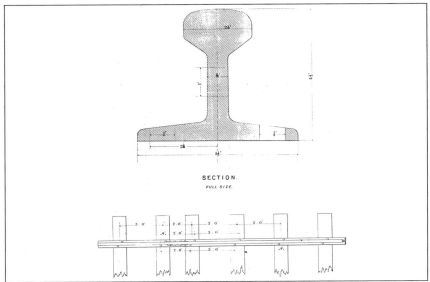

SECTION.
FULL SIZE.

Section of rail and plan of sleeper arrangements, Dockyard Railway 1873.

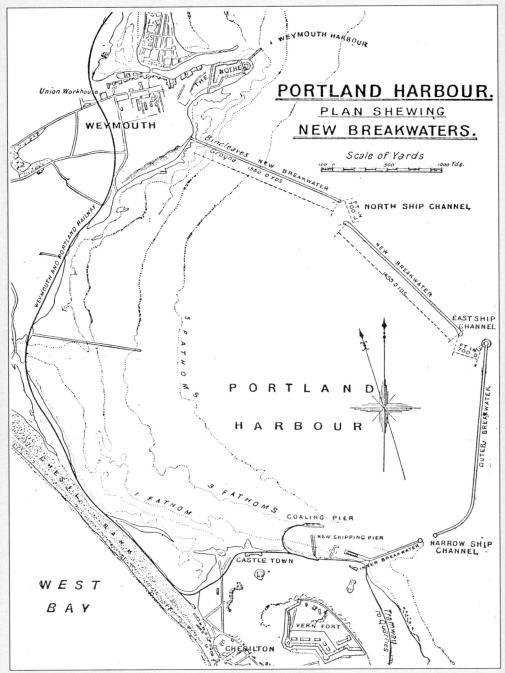

Plan showing the new breakwaters of the 1894 scheme. The Weymouth & Portland Railway can be seen running down the left side of the map, at Ferrybridge (unmarked) can be seen Whiteheads pier running out from the torpedo works.

A hand-operated crane used in the construction of the coaling pier during the early 1890s. In the background to the right is the Boys' Training ship *Boscawen*, to the left the old ironclad *Minotaur* relegated to training duties as *Boscawen II*.   *Southampton University Collection*

Early stages of construction work on the new coal jetty of 1893.   *Author's Collection*

Tip waggons used during the construction of the coaling pier, in the foreground a slotted post signal is part of the Dockyard railway system.   *Author's Collection*

The new coal pier of 1893 shortly after completion.   *Author's Collection*

The original stone tipping jetty around the turn of the century. Note the steam-operated gantry at the end for tipping the stone from the waggons into barges. In the background leading towards the dockyard gate no buildings have yet appeared; note the slotted post signal on the extreme left.
Author's Collection

The loading pier Portland Dockyard which replaced the original structure. Steam cranes are in action tipping truck loads of stone into barges ready to be towed out to the middle and northern breakwater arms then under construction. Behind the recently built coaling pier with hydraulic power house and cranes, in the distance are the coal hulks of the Channel Coaling Company.
Bill Macey Collection

Steam cranes on the stone-unloading jetty hoisting and tipping wagon loads of stone into barges
for transportation to the breakwater extension works.   *Author's Collection*

The development of the torpedo had undermined the defence works at Portland, ships at anchor in the roads now being sitting targets in the event of an attack. To protect the harbour two new 'defensive breakwaters' were constructed to enclose the two mile gap between the Breakwater Fort and a point between the Nothe and Sandsfoot Castle on the Weymouth side. So desperate was the need to carry out some form of protection that seven timber dolphins were constructed six to eight hundred yards apart linked with heavy wire cables and anti-torpedo nets as a temporary measure, these being in position by 1896.

The method of constructing the new breakwaters was to differ from the old, no timber staging was to be used. Stone was brought down to the Dockyard where it was loaded into special barges which were towed to the breakwater site for unloading either through bottom doors onto the sea-bed, or, in the case of large blocks above sea level, lifted off by crane.

The Government ordered work to commence in 1894, using direct labour together with convict labour in the quarries, and in September the following year a contract was signed with Messrs Steward's & Company for the supply of two million tons of rough stone. Three years later, following a change of Government, the entire work was handed over to Messrs Hill & Company of Gosport, and the £27,000 damages awarded to Steward's for the loss of the stone contract was, under Government pressure, overturned by the Appeal Court, leaving the quarry company nothing!

Convict labour was still retained in the quarries, and work progressed rapidly. By the middle of April 1899 the new breakwater had been raised up to low water level, this being achieved five months ahead of contract time. Again (as with the original breakwater) several captains were oblivious of its existence at high tide, and as the tide receded found their ships astride the new works!

Despite the use of more modern equipment, there were still accidents to both machinery and men during the construction work. On 3rd October, 1898 the cable parted on the top incline, the wagons running away and causing damage to the centre drum. On Tuesday 15th October, 1901 it was noted in the *Southern Times* that, owing to a coupling breaking, four loaded and four unloaded wagons on the incline ran out of control. The empty wagons were smashed to matchwood as a result of their escape, but the brakedrum slowed the loaded ones up and they were only slightly damaged. Frank Henry Churchill, a lad of 16 years employed by Messrs Hill as fireman on one of their engines, died as a result of being run over by the locomotive and a truck in September 1903. From the inquest report it would appear that he left the engine to free a chain attached to the wagon, and in the process of doing this was pushed by the buffer under the train which was still moving.

The Weymouth end of the breakwater was at Bincleaves, where the Great Western Railway had carried out considerable reclamation work before abandoning its proposed dock scheme. This land was taken over by the Admiralty and later became the site of a torpedo testing establishment. In March 1908 the lighthouse on the centre arm was brought into use, although work continued for several years in building up the breakwater before it was complete. As this was proceeding other work was being carried out to bring the shore establishments up to the required standards. The coaling facilities were

A pre-1905 view of the coaling jetty. In the foreground is the stone loading jetty for work on the breakwater extensions, and in the background boys' training ships. To the left *Boscawen* (ex-HMS *Trafalgar* (1841). To the right the ironclad *Minotaur* (1867) reduced to training duties as *Boscawen II*, whilst in the centre is *Agincourt* (1868) as *Boscawen III*. At the opening of the breakwater in 1872 these two ships were present as first class units of the fleet.

Author's Collection

Work in progress on building the northern arm of the breakwater, Weymouth is visible in the background. One of the temporary wooden dolphins constructed for defence purposes is clearly shown.   *W. Macey Collection*

Construction of the eastern breakwater arm, showing the steam crane that will lift stone from the barge (*far left*) to place in position on the breakwater. The basic equipment used in Victorian engineering works is well illustrated in this view.   *Author's Collection*

Ships' captains who failed to keep their charts up to date often had difficulties. The SS *Dinnington* (1874), whilst attempting to enter Portland Harbour during March 1901 ran onto the uncompleted centre arm, which at high tide was under water, leaving the vessel in the situation shown here as the tide receded. Later refloated the vessel was lost five years later on the Orkney Islands.   *M. Attwooll Collection*

Construction work taking place at the Bincleaves end of the two later breakwaters, at that stage a vast part of the northern arm was only just above sea level. Much of the land in the foreground and part of the bay to the left was to have been the site of the docks for the GWR Channel Island traffic. The structure on the island in the centre of the photograph is the original Admiralty torpedo testing establishment. Later the reclaimed foreground also became part of the establishment.   *British Railways*

again extended, a new Naval Hospital built, and the first of the oil tanks installed for what was rapidly to become the fuel of the future.

A much greater project than originally envisaged, the completed works formed the largest man-made harbour in the world, and were soon to prove their worth as storm clouds gathered towards the Great War.

However, long before its completion it had provided shelter for many vessels. Brunel's *Great Eastern*, following the fatal explosion on her trial trip down the Channel on 9th September, 1859, put into Portland for repairs. A week later on the 15th, her creator Isambard Kingdom Brunel passed away, and the mighty ship (like the massive breakwater) became an instant Victorian attraction, paddle steamers adding a visit to the vessel to the breakwater tour.

The Roadstead became the home of the training ship *Britannia* in 1862. On 29th September, 1863 she moved to the sheltered waters of the River Dart at Dartmouth, it being considered a superior place to train Britain's future admirals. In October 1866 the boys' training ship *Boscawen* arrived, a succession of vessels being used for this purpose until the early years of the present century. Britain's first armour plated battleship *Warrior* (1860) was the guard ship at Portland between 1875 and 1881 (this interesting vessel is now preserved as a floating museum at Portsmouth).

Marine technology and world events were fast overtaking the original concept of a simple harbour of refuge. With the introduction of steam power into the fleet Portland quickly became a coaling station for the Royal Navy, whilst in the north-west corner of the harbour coal hulks supplied vessels of the Merchant Navy calling *en voyage* to top up bunkers.

Before the turn of the century Portland had become the home of the Channel Fleet. In 1906 the Home Fleet established Portland as its base, from then until 1914 the finest ships of the world's largest navy could at times be seen at anchor. At 7 am on 29th July, 1914 the great fleet left Portland for the last time, proceeding to Scapa Flow in preparation for war.

To protect the harbour from possible torpedo and submarine attack boom defences were laid across the north and east entrances to the harbour, whilst on 4th November, 1914 the redundant battleship *Hood* (1893) was scuttled across the south entrance, where her hull remains to this day. Adding a sense of history to the event, she was the last British battleship to have a reduced freeboard (11 ft 3 in.), the last British Turret ship, and the ship on which bulge protection was first tested experimentally.

The economies following 1918 threatened the facilities at Portland, at one stage it being contemplated that (apart from fueling facilities) the base would close. A statement in 1923 read, 'Portland as far as can be foreseen, will on occasion be required as a naval anchorage for capital ships in a war with a Northern European power'. It was clear that Portland was too important for closure, and from December 1923 was known as 'HM Naval Base Portland', mainly being involved in the development of submarine and anti-submarine exercises. Again Portland became the anchorage for the Home Fleet and a backdrop for Naval reviews in 1932 and 1938. As another war approached the King reviewed the Reserve Fleet in Weymouth Bay on 9th August, 1939; of the 130 vessels present, 42 were to be lost in the forthcoming conflict.

4. *PORTLAND — The Harbour. — LL.*

Portland Dockyard showing the coal pier after the 1906 extension, with the Easton line in the foreground. Reclamation work is still proceeding, a portable

Looking down the Admiralty incline towards the lower drum, in the foreground can be seen the guide rollers and wire at the passing loop. *Weymouth & Portland Museum Services*

The middle drum of the Admiralty incline, a loaded waggon is hooked onto the wire ready to descend the final section of the incline. *Author's Collection*

The remains of 8 waggons at the foot of the Admiralty incline following the runaway of October 1901.   *Bill Macey Collection*

A general view of the stone stacking yard behind the prison at the Grove. In the foreground trucks stand at the top of a scree slope filling in quarried land. It was at this site Fox, Walker No. 332 went off the end of the track down the scree slope.   *E.A. Andrews Collection*

One of the Bagnall 0-4-0 saddle tanks working in the Convict Quarry, in the foreground a typical waggon used for the work. *Author's Collection*

Three types of waggon in use in the Convict Quarry, a flat bed, and waggon with open end, whilst behind a side-tipping type is seen at a higher level. *Author's Collection*

Block stacking yard near the Convict prison. As well as supplying the Portland project, large amounts of block stone were sent to other Government projects around the country. From 1884 stone was sent for a convict establishment and other works at Dover.   *Bill Macey Collection*

A general view of the Convict quarries looking south. Behind the steam crane are several houses in Grove Road. Partly obscured by the crane is one of the Bagnall 0-4-0 tanks and waggons employed on the breakwater contract. In the foreground convicts are at work with their warders standing guard.   *E.A. Andrews Collection*

Being vulnerable to attack by enemy aircraft, Portland was at first a very difficult harbour to defend, and not until the course of the war turned from the defensive to the offensive did it come into its own. Many clandestine cross-channel operations were carried out from Portland, and the harbour played a vital part in the build up to D-Day and the ending of the war.

When peace returned the harbour again became the base for the Home Fleet and training squadrons, but as time went by reductions in the fleet resulted in dockyard facilities being pruned towards the end of the 1950s, at which time the Royal Naval helicopter station opened to reflect the changing role of the Navy. As a training base it was often host to ships of other NATO countries. The submarine training squadron moved away, and it was not until the Falklands conflict of 1982 that Portland was again able to prove its worth in times of crisis, but by that time it was not served by a railway.

Returning to the 1890s, in order to carry out the breakwater extensions and other associated works, the Admiralty ordered four standard gauge 0-4-0 saddle tank locomotives from W.G. Bagnall of Stafford on 30th May, 1896. At that time Bagnall had constructed few standard gauge locomotives, in fact only fifty were produced up to 1914!

The four locomotives ordered were promised for delivery in 10 weeks, which would have been mid-August 1896, however Nos. 1493/4 did not leave Stafford until Christmas Eve, whilst Nos. 1495/6 followed on 20th February, 1897. Ten weeks would at best have been a short time to construct and supply four engines to special order and of the high standard specified.

The outside cylinders had a bore of 10 in., a stroke of 15 in. and the driving wheels a diameter of 2 ft 9 in. and a wheel base of 4 ft 9 in., a water tank capacity of 300 gallons, the boilers having copper fireboxes and brass tubes. The boiler pressure was 140 psi, and a tractive effort of 5,409 lb. Each locomotive was fitted with a steam brake, a live steam injector, and an axle driven pump.

During 1898 the locomotives were taken over by W. Hill & Company, according to a note in the Bagnall order book.

Two Peckett 0-4-0 saddle tanks, Nos. 686/7, arrived early in 1898. These engines weighed 21 tons, and had 12 in. diameter cylinders with a stroke of 18 in., and the diameter of the driving wheels was 2 ft 11 in. - slightly larger than the Bagnalls.

For heavier work large locomotives were required, and Peckett No. 751 was delivered new in 1898. Weighing 34 tons, she was an 0-6-0 saddle tank with outside cylinders of 14 in. diameter, 20 in. stroke, and 3 ft 7 in. diameter driving wheels. A second-hand engine was also acquired in the same year, Fox, Walker 0-4-0 saddle tank, No. 332, built in 1877 and named *Jessie*. She was purchased from Thomas Rigley of Windsor Bridge, having been used on the Manchester Ship Canal contract. At Portland she achieved notoriety when she slipped off the end of the track and down a scree slope whilst tipping rubble into a quarry near the prison.

A further second-hand engine was Manning, Wardle No. 503, built in July 1875. An 0-4-0 saddle tank weighing 19½ tons, she had 13 in. diameter cylinders with 18 in. stroke and 3 ft driving wheels. Before working at Portland she had been employed by Silverdale Ironworks & Collieries under the name of *Peplow*.

A typical period postcard view of the Convict quarries.   *Author's Collection*

Work proceeding in the Convict Quarry, in the foreground to the right a prison warder stands guard, note his sword. Also to prevent escapes a ring of armed soldiers surrounded the edge of the quarry. Note the two types of railway wagon in use, and behind the leg of the crane a vertical steam boiler can be seen.   *Author's Collection*

The rebuilding during 1907 of the viaduct leading to the old coal store (*far right*) in Portland Dockyard, a site to many known as 'Monkey Island'. The line below the viaduct ran out to the lower section of the inner breakwater. The square chimney in the centre belonged to the foundry, whilst behind to the left was the office of the Dockyard Engineer. *Author's Collection*

Steam cranes and other equipment lying at Castletown awaiting sale at the end of Hill's contracts at Portland. Several of the steam cranes were purchased by the quarry companies.
P. Trim Collection

A slotted post signal within the dockyard railway system, behind contractors' waggons in use during the construction of the coaling pier.

A slotted post signal of early design, the finial being of the unique design used by Stevens & Company, signal contractors.

Author's Collection

By the turn of the century nine locomotives were employed on the contract, but as the work decreased they were sold off. Peckett No. 686 was purchased by the Admiralty in 1904 and transferred to work on the breakwater at Fort Grosnez, Alderney. Shortly after her arrival she was involved in a spectacular accident during the Winter of 1911/12. Owing to a mixture of seaweed and water on the rails during rough weather, the engine failed to stop and - complete with her train of wagons - slid off the end of the breakwater into the sea, the crew jumping to safety at the last minute.

Within weeks the engine was salvaged, the cab, steam dome cover and chimney having been lost in the incident. The only other damage was to the smokebox and saddle tank. Following repairs the locomotive was soon back in service. During the early 1920s the line was leased and taken over by the Channel Island Granite Company Limited, a company owned by Brookes of Halifax. No. 686 continued to work until the German occupation of June 1940, the line being closed in September 1941 and falling into disuse. During 1943 the engine was reported as lying out of use on the quayside, and by the following year she had been shipped to Cherbourg where she was scrapped.

With the completion of the works at Portland, surplus engines were sold at Portland with other plant on 9th June, 1909. By 1911 Peckett 0-6-0 No. 751 had passed to J. Pugsley of Bristol, a plant contractor, who resold it to the Ebbw Vale Iron & Steel Company, Finsdon Park Ironstone Pits, Northants. Following several moves within that company, including one to South Wales, she was scrapped in August 1957. The Manning, Wardle No. 503 had also passed to Joseph Pugsley for further service.

Three Bagnalls, Nos. 1494, 1495, 1496, and Peckett 687 reverted to the Admiralty, whilst Bagnall No. 1493 remained with Hill & Company having moved to Brixham, Devon, to assist with the breakwater extensions there.

In August 1916 the plant from that contract was sold. No. 1493 passed to the Ministry of Munitions, who arranged for the engine to be returned to Bagnall's for rebuilding. This mainly consisted of work on the boiler, including a new smokebox and tube plate, new tubes, and repairs to the firebox.

By March 1917 the engine had been sent to Watford Explosives Factory where she was employed as *Nog 2*. With the closure of the factory following the Great War, No. 1493 was put up for sale on 21st February, 1920, from which time any definitive details are not known.

Pressure of work during the Great War required an additional engine at Portland, resulting in the delivery of Andrew Barclay 0-4-0 saddle tank No. 1570, built in September 1917. Fitted with 14 in. diameter cylinders and a stroke of 22 in. and 3 ft 5 in. driving wheels, her weight was 22 tons.

Of the three Bagnalls taken over by the Admiralty, two were sold in 1925 to James Smith & Company of Hamworthy, Poole, who it would appear at the time were acting as a dealers.

No. 1495 passed to the Hastings and St Leonards Gas Company for use at their Glyne Gap Works. There her duties continued until the arrival of a diesel shunter in 1953. The following June, No. 1495 was scrapped by Messrs Cohen.

No. 1496 was purchased locally by the Hamworthy Wharf and Coal Company Ltd, moving to West Shore Wharf, Hamworthy. Retaining her old number, 4, she was named *Iris*. During her career at Hamworthy her owners become Stephenson, Clarke

Brand new and highly polished Peckett No. 5 stands with her attendants. The epitome of the Victorian industrial locomotive, everything is in place including the oil can. Later serving the Admiralty Fort and Breakwater at Grosnez Alderney, her fate was sealed during the German occupation.

Bill Macey Collection

Former Portland Dockyard Peckett No. 686. Seen here in Mannez Quarry, Alderney about 1922. The different cab and chimney following her fall into the sea are clearly shown.

E.A. Brooke, courtesy S.A. Leleux

Peckett No. 686 stands with her crew whilst working on the Alderney Breakwater Railway. Having arrived on the island in 1904, she was involved in a accident in the winter of 1911 when after slipping on wet rails she plunged over the edge of the breakwater and lay submerged for several weeks. After recovery she was fitted with a new chimney and reconstructed cab as shown in this photograph.   *R.W. Kidner Collection*

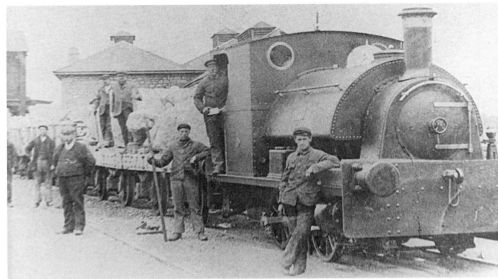

A Bagnall 0-4-0 tank poses for the photographer with its train of stone before shunting it back under the top drum of the Admiralty incline, seen on the extreme left of the photograph. In the background are the engine sheds and workshop used by locomotives working in the quarries at the top of the incline.   *Peter Trim Collection*

Bagnall No. 1494 in original condition with open cab. With her crew in attendance, she stands at the approach to the loading pier.   *Author's Collection*

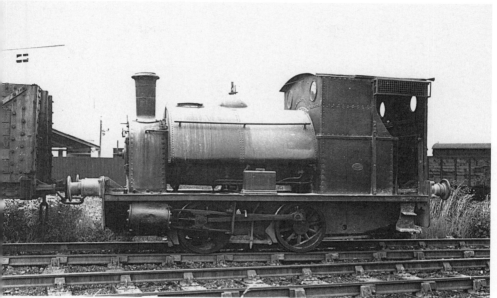

Bagnall No. 1494 at Kirby Thore Plaster Works in August 1952, near the end of its working life of 56 years, and three owners. By that time various alterations had taken place including the fitting of a complete cab.

Frank Jones

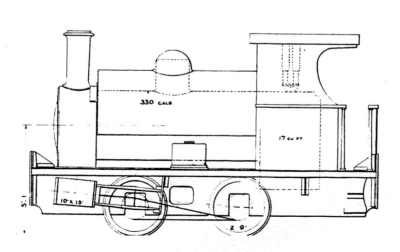

Bagnall Locomotives Nos. 1493-1496

Fox, Walker No. 332 after having fallen from the end of the track down the scree slope at the rear
of the prison.   *Author's Collection*

Andrew Barclay No. 1570 photographed on 11th March, 1961, alongside Fowler diesel shunter
No. 111.   *C.L. Caddy*

& Associated Companies Ltd, and later Southern Wharves Ltd, Hamworthy. Replaced by a new locomotive, No. 1496 was scrapped by Baker of Southampton during 1950.

Having reviewed the history of the majority of the engines employed on the breakwater and within the Dockyard, we return to just before the turn of the century, at which point the history of the section of line from the actual Dockyard to its junction with the Weymouth & Portland line at Castletown Sidings becomes a little involved with the Easton & Church Hope Railway, and this section is covered in more detail in Volume Two of this history. The signalling which had been installed within the Dockyard had at some time fallen into disuse, as a letter from the Engineer of the Easton company in January 1899 stated that the signal box at the Dockyard (Portland No. 2) had to be removed to allow for the completion of the Easton line, and it was apparent that it had not been used for a great number of years. Later the same month the Admiralty authorised the Great Western Railway to remove the signal box as soon as possible. The track was also a little below the required standards. The ballast needed building up where it had been trampled down by horses and the original Vignoles rails needed replacing, together with the bridge over the 'Merchants' incline' at Castletown. The agreement of 1874 concerning the operating of the line by the railway companies was also terminated at the end of 1898.

These alterations were made to allow the completion of the Easton & Church Hope Railway. An agreement signed in June 1906 recited that,

> If the Admiralty at any time require the railway companies to provide an engine or engines for the purpose of shunts or other work at the Breakwater Naval Establishment, the Companies shall at reasonable notice, if an engine is available at Portland, charge 8s. per hour per engine, minimum charge 8s., extra charge of 10s. per engine if obtained from Weymouth. If engine had to be specially lit up: £2.

In 1907 it was decided to raise the height of the northern arm of the breakwater, the contract being awarded again to Messrs Hill & Co. Again the Dockyard railway was fully employed as thousands of tons of stone were shipped across the harbour for the project.

By the time the construction of the system was completed the railway in the Dockyard extended to most piers and other sites. This was the age of industrial railways, which were not only used for handling traffic brought in by the main line railway systems, but also for internal movements.

During World War I provision was made for ambulance trains to use various jetties within the yard and the following special instructions were laid down for their operation.

> The whole of the hand signalling to control the movements of the train over the dockyard lines must be done by the Railway Companies' staff and the Admiralty staff will place the various switches on the lines over which the train is to pass in the correct position and secure them with the wooden plugs which have been provided. Before trains are taken over the dockyard lines, an assurance should be given to the Railway Companies' inspector or other person in charge that this has been duly attended to.
>
> When the trains have entered the Dockyard they will be brought to a stand clear of the connection leading to the coal jetty, about 40 yards from the entrance gate at the junction with the Portland and Easton main line.

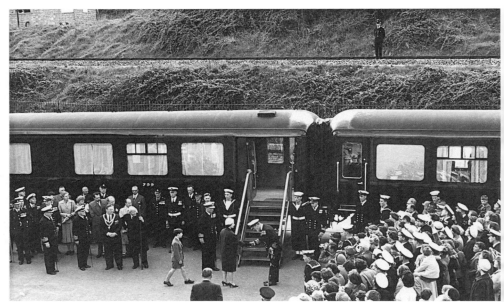

Her Majesty the Queen followed by HRH Prince Charles, board the Royal train in Portland Dockyard on 29th April, 1959.   *M.J. Tattershall Collection*

Andrew Barclay No. 8, decorated in traditional style for Navy days, 20th May, 1961. This was the only occasion when the general public could ride over the remains of the Breakwater Railway, it was also the last occasion when a steam locomotive would be used for such an event.
                                                                                    C.L. Caddy

If a train is required at once to be taken to the jetty head, alongside which the hospital ships will be berthed, two or more of the Admiralty dockyard engines will be attached to it - in the case of two engines, one at the front and the other at the rear, and if three engines are employed, two at the front and one at rear - will take it to the necessary position opposite the ship, and after the wounded have been loaded will return with the train to the spot from which they started with it, when the Railway Companies' engines will be attached to it and work away.

Should it be found necessary to berth the special trains in the dockyard to await the arrival of the hospital ship, or to take their turn in loading, the Admiralty foreman will point out to the Railway Companies' staff where such berthing shall be done and the trains will be moved into the required positions by the Railway Companies' engines or the dockyard engines, as may be most desirable, and will thereafter be worked to the coal jetty by the dockyard engines in the manner before shown.

Also included in the instructions was a set of whistle codes and other points of guidance to staff operating in the confines of the Dockyard.

Over the years there was always a small amount of stone required to top up the breakwater and the incline and quarry lines remained in use for this - albeit to a very limited extent - and an engine was kept in the shed at the top of the incline for the purpose. In 1921 the prison became a Borstal Institution. It being considered that quarry work was unsuitable for Borstal boys, the quarry and masonry works were closed. A small amount of stone was removed by direct labour until the mid-1930s, when it was decided to allow the stone companies to supply material for this work under a contract which included delivery to the Dockyard. After this contract came into force the Admiralty quarry closed, the engine was brought down from the top and the rails and brake drums removed from the incline. The remainder of the Dockyard railway continued to operate carrying the stores and equipment required by the Navy.

No. 1494, the remaining Bagnall at Portland was noted as being out of use by April 1937. It is generally considered that she was the last engine employed in the Convict Quarry at the top of the incline.

In May 1939 she was offered for sale at £500 by Matthews & Wood, steel and iron merchants of Newport, Mon., and was purchased later in the year by the Barrow Haematite Steel Company of Barrow-in-Furness. There is no evidence that the engine ever went to Newport, but on her journey to Barrow which was undertaken being towed as part of a normal freight train she had to be removed at Shrewsbury, no doubt caused by a 'hot box'.

In the ownership of Barrow Steel as No. 12 she moved to various sites. In 1940 she was employed in Devonshire Limestone Quarry, and after October 1942 at Pennington Ore Mill, later moving to Stainton. At the end of 1946 she was advertised for sale through dealers Abelson of Birmingham for £400. In January 1947 the engine was acquired by Thomas Mcghie & Sons of the Thistle Plaster Works, Kirkby Thore, Westmorland, where she remained until scrapped in 1953.

During World War II the work in the yard was handled by the remaining Peckett, No. 687, and Andrew Barclay 0-4-0 saddle tank No. 1570, built in September 1917. The latter had 14 in. diameter cylinders with a stroke of 22 in. She was fitted with 3 ft 5 in. driving wheels and her weight was 22 tons.

This situation continued until 1959 when Peckett 687 was withdrawn from service. Having been fitted with a new boiler supplied by Bagnall in 1938, No.

Admiralty Quarry engine shed and workshops at the top of the Admiralty incline, used by locomotives working in the Admiralty Quarries. Still standing over 60 years after the Admiralty incline and quarry lines closed.   *Author*

The greatest memorial to the Admiralty Railway is the breakwater, the reason for the railway's construction. The fort at the outer end of the original breakwater is viewed from the air on 9th November, 1976. The later buildings that were added can be clearly seen, as can the small breakwater to protect the supply vessels.   *HMS Osprey Photographic Section*

687 had given 61 years service to Portland Dockyard through construction, peace, and war. Although after 1939 only two locomotives served the yard, the question of engine shortage hardly arose; as many items in a dockyard were of a bulky nature, the tracks were also shared with the many steam cranes which served the establishment. Given a length of rope or chain a steam crane makes a reasonable substitute engine, as does a motor lorry. However, that was in the days before Health & Safety, when a little ingenuity saved the day!

During the late 1950s the decline in the activities at the Naval base was having a marked effect upon the number of people employed, and the use of the Dockyard Railway. The last event of note took place on Wednesday 29th April, 1959 when following a visit to HMS *Eagle*, Her Majesty The Queen accompanied by Prince Charles joined the Royal Train in the Dockyard.

After servicing at Weymouth the Royal Train was taken empty to Portland, travelling between Portland station and the dockyard entrance with an engine at each end. At the Dockyard gate the leading engine was uncoupled and went ahead onto the Easton line whilst the rear locomotive pushed the train into the Dockyard. The leading engine then came onto the front of the train. At 3 pm the train departed, climbing the stiff gradient out of the dockyard. It was to be the last passenger train to leave the Dockyard, and the last Royal Train to travel over the Portland branch.

In December 1960 two Fowler 0-4-0 diesel shunters from the Admiralty depot at Bisley, Lancs., arrived at Portland - No. 22920 built in 1940, and 22935, built in 1941. They carried yard Nos. 11 and 114 respectively. The end was now fast approaching for steam traction within the yard, and the Peckett - the last survivor of the original nine locomotives - was broken up, whilst the Barclay was last in steam during Navy Days at Whitsun 1961 when, wearing the traditional long funnel and other decorations, she gave rides in an open wagon along part of the Breakwater Railway. She then lay out of use and neglected until Tuesday 14th January, 1963, when she was loaded onto a low loader and transported to a scrapyard at Ringwood to be broken up.

The two diesels were active until the closure of the Portland branch in April 1965, after which they lay idle until 1967 when they were sold. No.111 went to Axminster where she was used by the contractors removing the Lyme Regis branch, before going to Bird's Commercial Motors of Long Marston. No. 113 went direct to Bird's yard at Pontymister, Mon. (now Gwent), thus ending the story of railways on Portland Breakwater and Dockyard.

Breakwater and Dockyard Locomotives

J.T. Leather, Contractor

No.	Type	Builder/ Works No.	Built	Cylinders	Wheel dia.	Weight	Note
	0-4-0 WT	EBW 329	1852?	10½ in. x 17 in.	4 ft		2
	0-4-0 WT	EBW 454	1853				1
	0-4-0 WT	EBW					1
	0-4-0 WT	EBW					1
	0-4-0 WT	EBW					1

1. Upon completion of Breakwater work sold to I.W. Boulton Ashton-under-Lyme.

2. Named QUEEN, 1868 sold to Torbay & Brixham Railway, 1879 South Devon Railway, 1883 Great Western Railway, scrapped.

W. Hill & Company, Contractors

No.	Type	Builder/ Works No.	Built	Cylinders	Wheel dia.	Weight	Note
1	0-4-0 ST	BAG 1493	1896	10 in. x 15 in.	2 ft 9 in.	16 t 10 cwt	5
2	0-4-0 ST	BAG 1494	1896	10 in. x 15 in.	2 ft 9 in.	16 t 10 cwt	1
3	0-4-0 ST	BAG 1495	1897	10 in. x 15 in.	2 ft 9 in.	16 t 10 cwt	1
4	0-4-0 ST	BAG 1496	1897	10 in. x 15 in.	2 ft 9 in.	16 t 10 cwt	1
5	0-4-0 ST	PEC 686	1898	12 in. x 18 in.	2 ft 11 in.	21 t	2
6	0-4-0 ST	PEC 687	1898	12 in. x 18 in.	2 ft 11 in.	21 t	1
	0-6-0 ST	PEC 751	1898	14 in. x 20 in.	3 ft 7 in.	34 t	3
	0-4-0 ST	FW 332	1877				6
	0-4-0 ST	MW 503	1875	13 in. x 18 in.	3 ft	19 t 10 cwt	4 7

1 To Admiralty Portland
2 To Admiralty 1904 transferred to Alderney
   Breakwater scrapped 1940
3 To Pugsley Bristol 1911, to Ebbw Vale Iron &
   Steel, scrapped 1957
4 Ex-Silverdale Iron works.

5 To Brixham Breakwater work (Hill), 1917
   Min. Munitions Watford.
6 Ex-Rigley Manchester
7 To Pugsley Bristol

The Admiralty, Portland Dockyard

No.	Type	Builder/ Works No.	Built	Cylinders	Wheel dia.	Weight	Note
2	0-4-0 ST	BAG 1494	1896	10 in. x 15 in.	2 ft 9 in.	16 t 10 cwt	1 4
3	0-4-0 ST	BAG 1495	1897	10 in. x 15 in.	2 ft 9 in.	16 t 10 cwt	1 2
4	0-4-0 ST	BAG 1496	1897	10 in. x 15 in.	2 ft 9 in.	16 t 10 cwt	1 3
6	0-4-0 ST	PEC 687	1898	12 in. x 18 in.	2 ft 11 in.	21 t	1 5
8	0-4-0 ST	AB 1570	1917	14 in. x 22 in.	3 ft 5 in.	22 t	6
111	0-4-0 DM	JF 22920	1940				7 8
113	0-4-0 DM	JF 22935	1941				9

1 Ex-W. Hill Portland Dockyard contract.
2 To J. Smith Hamworthy 1925, to Hastings &
   St Leonards Gas Company, Glyne Gap Gas
   Works. Scrapped on site June 1954 by Cohen.
3 To J. Smith Hamworthy, to Hamworthy
   Wharf & Coal Co. Scrapped 1950 by Baker of
   Southampton.
4 To To Mathews & Wood Newport 1939, to
   Barrow Steel 1939, to Thistle Plaster Works,
   Kirkby Thore 1947, scrapped 1953.

5 Scrapped locally circa 1959.
6 To J. Ward breakers, Ringwood, January 1963
   (still in Ringwood yard at end of October).
7 Ex-Admiralty Depot Bisley Lancs, 1960.
8 To contractors removing Lyme Regis branch
   1967, to Bird's Pontymister.
9 To Bird's Yard, Long Marston 1967.

Chapter Four

Other Minor Railways and Associated Equipment

Apart from the 'Merchants' (or Portland) Railway, there were several other small rail systems on the Island used by the stone industry. Some were little more than a couple of lengths of rail, but others ran a considerable distance. By their very nature they tended to come and go as quarry work progressed or was given up at any particular site.

The majority of these lines were feeders connected to the main 'Merchants' Railway', and as quarrying extended further into the island they were constructed to remove the stone. By the mid-1800s they had become quite extensive, particularly in the area north of Reforne and Easton. Lines were laid to Under Waycroft when quarrying operations commenced there, and were later extended to the west and south of this area and into Maggot Quarry (this being near where Steward's built their sawmills in Easton lane, the offices with their modern extension still standing). Extensions were laid across Easton Lane when the east side of Inmosthay was opened up for quarrying. A line ran southwards parallel to Easton Lane and close to what was later to become the end of the Easton & Church Hope Railway, it then turned west behind Reforne passing through what later became the railway coal yard and Jordon (later the YMCA cricket pitch). Crossing Wide Street it proceeded alongside the north wall of St George's cemetery descending to quarries at Goslands and Bowers.

A connection was made with the Portland Railway between Priory Corner and the Rectory, having come from the north end of Inmosthay via a tunnel under the road at Yeates.

By the mid-1850s lines had been established from Priory Corner across to West Cliff, some being constructed by the Lano family. As these continued eastward spurs were added - several passing under well constructed 'dry stone' arches and two tunnels took lines eastwards under Wide Street into Inmosthay. So extensive were the workings in that area that four tunnels existed under Wide Street alone. On the east side of Easton Lane lines were added to make connections with the Admiralty Quarries, although owing to the difference in gauge any transfer of stone was carried out by crane. To the west of Easton Lane, following the opening of the Easton & Church Hope Railway to goods traffic in 1900, a gantry was erected over the cutting at the end of the line allowing stone to be transferred from Steward's railway to standard gauge wagons in the cutting below. Of the feeder lines Steward's railway was the largest. At its peak it consisted of five miles of track!

Other quarry owners operated their own railway systems, including W.H.P. Weston, of Weston Quarries. As with Messrs Barnes and Steward's, these lines eventually came under the ownership of the Bath & Portland Stone Firms. There appeared to be little difficulty for the local quarry owners in obtaining permission either to tunnel under or cross public roads with their lines, either in the days of the old Local Board or the later Urban District Council. After all, the 'Gaffers' of the quarry were members of the authority and stone was the

A simple bridge over the former trackwork of one of the lines running into the quarries north of Easton.   *M.J. Tattershall*

Built by J.C. Lano in 1854 this arch of dry stone construction has survived the railway and stands in Tout Quarry, near West Cliff. On this part of the system parts of the line were at two levels, the lower line taking quarried stone out towards the Portland Railway, whilst the upper line usually went to the cliff face where waste materials were dumped.   *M.J. Tattershall*

staple industry!   In April 1892 the owners of Weston Quarries asked for permission to carry a tram line under the main road at Southwell.   This necessitated the road being raised at that point, but the application was granted.

In February 1900 F.J. Barnes applied for permission to place tram lines in Wide Street and Southwell, and again permission was granted.   At the same meeting a Mr Lynham applied for permission to place two bay windows in houses in New Street. It appears that these were not shown in the original plans and consequently permission was refused, proving that Town Hall bureaucracy is nothing new!

The breakwater contractor (Messrs Hill) extended its line south of Grove Road and this was of a more sophisticated nature than the earlier quarry lines, being of standard gauge and connected to the Admiralty system.

Also on site was an overhead cableway for the removal of stone. Operated by steam, it caused great interest at the time and was known as 'The Blondin' after the French acrobat and tightrope walker Charles Blondin (1824-1897). The *Southern Times* for 12th May, 1900 described it thus:

> The erection which is some 65 feet high, stands on four strong railway trolleys, and looks all the world like a scaffolding for a high chimney. The workmen engaged in erecting it tell you it is a 'Blondin' and is an American invention and the first of the kind erected in England. 'Blondin' suggests tightrope walking, and you are informed that is exactly the work of this machinery, only stone tubs will walk along it instead of men. The Blondin we understand to be capable of overcoming the difficulty of crane removal from place to place. An endless steel chain will run longitudinally through the quarry and lift out stone through the entire length. When the quarry has been worked the Blondin will be moved on railway lines to the next place to be quarried.

Contractors' locomotives have, by their nomadic existence, always been difficult to trace, and with many of the early examples definitive records are sadly lacking. For example, no details remain of the locomotive used by Messrs John Aird & Sons during the construction of the Weymouth & Portland Railway.

There are also few details of contractor's engines used during the construction of the Easton & Church Hope Railway. Between 1889 and 1895 Messrs Perry, Cutbill & De Lungo was contracted to construct the line, but unfortunately very little can be gleamed about either the company or its work from the records of the Easton & Church Hope company.

However, it is known that in February 1894 the Wotton Tramway had to pay £10 towards the cost of transporting Manning, Wardle 0-6-0 ST No. 616 from Portland to Quainton Road, via Nine Elms. No. 616 was of the 'K' type having two inside cylinders 12 in. by 17 in. and wheels of 3 ft 1⅛ in. diameter, the saddle tank holding 450 gallons. The engine weighed 18 tons loaded, and was fitted with brakes on all wheels. The crew were protected from the elements only by a spectacle plate.

New in July 1876, No. 616 was delivered to Messrs T.J. Waller of Manchester and named *Prestwich*, later passing to J.D. Nowell of Todmorden who renamed her *Huddersfield*. She was next recorded as working at Bridgwater for Messrs Cutbill, Son, & De Lungo. As Cutbill & De Lungo was working at Portland it has to be assumed that the engine moved to the island at some unrecorded date.

Manning, Wardle 0-6-0 ST No. 616, purchased by the Wotton Tramway in February 1895 from contractors at Portland. The many well known features of a Manning, Wardle locomotive are clearly shown in this view taken at Quainton Road, junction of the tramway.

Ken Jones Collection

Contractor's engine *Hornby* stands on the Easton & Church Hope Line alongside the dockyard. As the engine does not have its coupling rods fitted, it is assumed she has either just arrived to commence work or is about to depart. *Hornby*, Manning, Wardle 'L' type No. 1211 was constructed in 1891 and having passed through various owners was finally scrapped in 1932.

Author's Collection

The Wotton Tramway (The Brill branch) was originally going to hire the engine at £26 a month, but Earl Temple, the company Chairman and the tramway's benefactor, purchased it outright for £450. However, £50 had to be spent on urgent repairs the following year. Still carrying the name *Huddersfield*, 616 continued to work the tramway until December 1899 when the Metropolitan Railway took over the line, *Huddersfield* then required rebuilding and valued at only £150, she was sold to Messrs Phillips of Emlyn Works, Newport (Mon.), and arrived at Gloucester for delivery on 18th June, 1901.

During 1895 Messrs Perry, Cutbill, & De Lungo was discharged from its contract with the Easton & Church Hope Railway. There was then, not for the first time, a pause in the progress of the railway.

On 30th July, 1897 Messrs Packman, Popkiss & Heasman took over as engineers to the Easton company, and H.M. Keone became the contractor. In a letter dated 22nd October, 1897 from H.M. Keone to Packman, Popkiss, & Heasman it was stated that 'one engine has been purchased and is being fitted up to be provided as early as possible. Meanwhile we are proceeding with the work by horse traction'. On 8th November Packman, Popkiss & Heasman informed the Easton company that 'a locomotive and travelling crane are expected early this week'. A fourth letter on the 30th reported, 'no locomotive yet, expected next week'.

However a letter sent on 6th December reported that the engine, whilst on its way to Portland as part of a normal goods train (a frequent practice at that period) had suffered a broken axle, and was moved to Northam engine shed at Southampton on the LSWR to await a replacement. The Minute books of the Easton company recorded that an engine commenced work in January 1898.

At this point the chain of events becomes confused, a letter from Mr E.J. Ashwell (who we assume was on site) to Messrs Popkiss on 8th February, 1898, stating, 'More tip wagons have arrived at Portland station, and another locomotive is on the way, expected next week'. Another letter on the 14th from Popkiss, stated, 'Two locomotives and tip wagons on the way'.

A second engine is not mentioned in the Minute books until July, when Mr Lano complained that there was a risk of his hayricks catching fire owing to sparks from the 'engines'.

Thanks to the photographer we have evidence of one engine used during the final stages of the construction; *Hornby*, a Manning, Wardle 'L' type 0-6-0ST built in May 1891, maker's No. 1211, fitted with two cylinders of 12 in. diameter with a stroke of 18 in. and 3 ft driving wheels.

Supplied new to contractor Messrs Ecklersley, Godfrey, & Liddelow, of Liverpool and named *Hornby*, she was used in the construction of the No. 1 Branch Dock of the Canada Dock (Liverpool) for the Mersey Docks & Harbour Board. By late 1893, No. 1211 was employed by Pethick Bros in the construction of the Vale of Glamorgan line of the Barry Railway, moving to Portland some time during 1898.

A letter to the Easton company on 11th September, 1899 stated that the sub-contractor had been removed from the works. The next reference to H.M. Keone was in adverts for the sale of contractors' plant, re H.M. Keone in liquidation, Easton & Church Hope Railway, by auction on 15th February, 1901.

Working in the quarries of F.J. Barnes Ltd is 0-4-2 wing tank *Excelsior*, complete with tip waggons. The driver is thought to be 'Scottie' Mackenzie.   *J.H. Lucking Collection*

Tipping spoil over West Cliff, *Excelsior* stands well clear and is attended by her driver.
                                                                              J.H. Lucking Collection

The lots included two Manning, Wardle engines (an 0-6-0 12 in., and an 0-4-0 10 in.), 60 side and end tip wagons, steam and hand derrick cranes, 200 tons of rails (54 lb. per yard), points and crossings, and a Jubilee Decauville railway and wagons.

The 0-6-0 is almost definitely *Hornby*, the 0-4-0 most likely a Manning, Wardle 'F' type with 10 in. by 16 in. cylinders, a type very popular with contractors, but no firm details have come to light. *Hornby* next appeared in the ownership of Herbert Weldon of Birmingham who had a contract for widening the Aberbeeg to Llanhilleth section of the GWR between 1898-1902. Later purchased by Pauling & Company, as No. 75 she was employed in the construction of the Gerrards Cross-High Wycombe section of the GWR and Great Central Joint Line. Passing then to J.F. Wake Dealers of Darlington the engine was rebuilt. In 1916 she was sold to J. & J. Charlesworth Ltd, for use in collieries south-east of Leeds, where she remained until broken up by Hunslet of Leeds in 1932, thus bringing to an end the story of a common contractor's engine that became involved in the complexity of the Easton & Church Hope Railway.

The quarry railways only once moved away from horse traction, when Messrs Barnes opened a 2 ft gauge line between West Cliff and Trade and Slidcroft quarries. It was later moved to near Weston Corner serving Barley Croft and Grain Croft quarries, the line then proceeding westwards to the cliff edge at Mutton Cove, south of Blacknore Point. The purpose of this line was to facilitate the dumping of spoil over the cliff. The wagons were of the side-tipping type, and were hauled by a small steam locomotive named *Excelsior* which had an interesting career before arriving on Portland.

Ordered in February 1888 from W.G. Bagnall of Stafford as Works No. 970, she was delivered in April of the same year to Christopher J. Naylor of Bryn-Llywarch Hall Estate, mid-Wales, to operate on a line about three miles long to Kerry station on the Cambrian Railway. The principal use of this narrow gauge system was to transport timber and other estate products to the station.

This little 0-4-2 wing tank engine weighed only 3 tons 15 cwt. in working order. The two cylinders had a diameter of 5 in. with a piston stroke of 7½ in., the driving wheels being 1 ft 3¼ in. diameter and the bogie wheels 10 in. The tractive effort developed was 1,290 lb. The estate railway closed in April 1895, the stock and locomotive being sold to Messrs James Nuttall & Sons contractors, of Manchester, who used *Excelsior* during the construction of the Lynton & Barnstaple narrow gauge railway in North Devon. Upon completion of this work in May 1898, the engine was purchased by F.J. Barnes of Portland and put to work on the quarry tip line. *Excelsior* was built with a balloon-type spark-arresting chimney and open back cab, but during her stay in Devon a stove-pipe chimney was fitted and a crude extension to the cab added, and she was in this condition when she arrived at Portland. From photographs it would appear that the cab extension (which, whilst at Portland, consisted of corrugated iron sheeting) was removed during the summer months. When her work at Portland was done she lay idle until cut up in the yard of Barnes Foundry which then existed behind Easton Square.

The only other steam-operated line was the siding extension towards Southwell from Easton station. This line was in fact part of the original Easton

Excelsior - W.G. Bagnall Works No. 970 of 1888

Based on known dimensions and photographs of No. 970 and contemporary Bagnall products. Apart from wheelbase, gauge and wheel diameters, no other dimensions can be guaranteed.

Scale 1:43.5 Drawn by Roy C. Link © 1990.

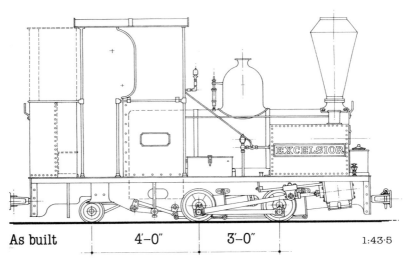

As built   4'-0"   3'-0"   1:43·5

Drawing A - Right-hand side elevation showing the locomotive as built. The dotted lines at the bunker end show the cab enclosure fitted when working on the construction of the Lynton & Barnstaple Railway.

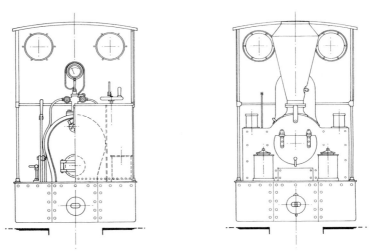

Drawing B and C - Front and rear elevations as built. Cab fittings are based on contemporary Bagnall practice. Note access door to spark arrestor on one side only.

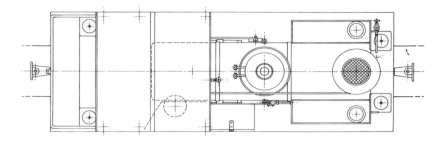

Drawing D - Plan view as built. Note that whistle is off centre. One only of later 'Roscoe' pattern lubricators shown. As built only oil cups were fitted. Note that rear 'bunker' may in fact have been a third water tank - as fitted to other Bagnall locomotives of the period. There is a side bunker in the cab space for coal.

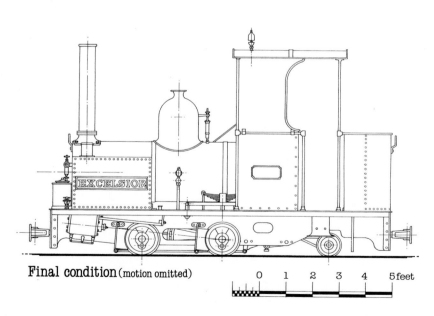

Final condition (motion omitted)

0 1 2 3 4 5 feet

Drawing E - Left-hand side view (motion omitted) of final condition with plain chimney and whistle repositioned on cab roof.

Above: Excelsior with train during loading operations. As the boards around the rear of the cab are missing this photograph must have been taken during the summer months.

Author's Collection

Right: A vertical-boilered steam operated channeller. The small steam engine on this rail-mounted machine can clearly be seen.

R. Twig Collection

& Church Hope Railway of 1867. Having left the Easton branch south of the station, the line known as Quarry Tip Siding climbed into the yard of what in later years became the South Western Stone Company. It then crossed the road opposite Pennsylvania Castle, just north of a point now known as Perryfield Corner, and continued beside the Southwell Road on the seaward side, on a low embankment, finally ending in a tip. Immediately after crossing Southwell Road there was a short siding serving a shed in which (it is assumed) the engine was stabled.

A visit to the line by Mr Arthur Lemon, the Easton & Church Hope Company Secretary, and officers of the LSWR in September 1912 revealed that the use of a locomotive on this section was not legally agreed with the Easton & Church Hope Railway who owned the line, although agreed by the joint operating companies who were charging 1d. a ton as a tipping charge! It appears that since the opening of the line it had come into use as a siding for tipping rubble over the edge of the cliff. The United Stone Firms Ltd had just opened a new quarry nearby and were making good use of quarry tip siding to dispose of their waste, using a small locomotive to haul the trucks of rubbish.

The condition of the siding was not good, much of the waste had been dumped on railway property instead of over the cliff, the rails in places had been roughly re-laid, and in one place were found to be four feet above their original level. The tip wagons of two ton capacity were being overloaded by almost 50 per cent.

From records available, the engine commenced work about the 18th September, 1912. How long it operated is not known and unfortunately research has failed to discover the identity of the locomotive used in this clandestine operation.

Further south along Southwell Road another standard gauge line crossed the road. On the seaward side it divided, one line going down a steep incline towards the sea, the other continuing at a higher level to form a loop which ended in two short spurs terminating at the cliff edge. To the north of the road crossing a stone building which was connected with this line still survives at the time of writing. Beyond this building the line spread out into Coombefield quarries.

There were several other short sections of line on the Island on which the wagons were either hauled by horses or just simply manhandled. One such line ran from a quarry behind the Eight Kings Public House at Southwell across the Portland Bill road and out towards the cliff.

For a number of years stone was quarried at Portland Bill, some of this stone being taken from the cliff edge thus forming a shelving effect. Two quarry owners were involved in this operation, Messrs F.J. Barnes and John Pearce, the latter commencing operations during 1889 on several plots of land. A quantity of this stone was shipped directly from the Bill, the blocks being loaded by hand crane into ships moored alongside the rocks. The last loads left in 1893, and the earthworks of a tramway can still be seen to the seaward side of the Lobster Pot restaurant, and also near the base of the present lighthouse which opened in January 1906. 'Bill' stone differed somewhat from that obtained from the main Island quarries, being a slightly brownish colour.

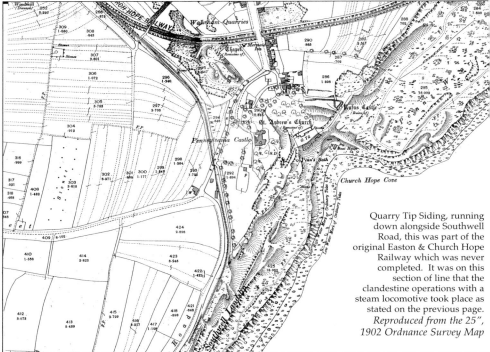

Quarry Tip Siding, running down alongside Southwell Road, this was part of the original Easton & Church Hope Railway which was never completed. It was on this section of line that the clandestine operations with a steam locomotive took place as stated on the previous page.
Reproduced from the 25", 1902 Ordnance Survey Map

Quarries along the cliff side between Southwell and Portland Bill, looking towards Southwell. Various cranes and narrow gauge railway line can be seen, in the bottom right-hand corner the chimney of a steam channeller can just be seen.   *K. Lynham Collection*

At the turn of the century the Island's stone railways were at their zenith covering all of 'Tophill' from Weston northwards to Priory Corner, and across the entire Island as far south as Easton. A majority of the feeder lines were removed during World War I, the traction engine taking their place as a more flexible form of transport between the quarry and the saw mills, the railhead of the 'Merchants' Railway' at Priory Corner, or the main line loading points on the Island.

Just as it took a number of years for the traction engine to replace the horse, the use of steam power in the quarry industry was also slow in coming. By the late 1880s steam engines were beginning to be employed in the various mills. When Barnes took over the Portland Stone Company yard adjoining the railway in Victoria Square, new machinery was introduced, in the form of six new frame saws patented by Cox of Weymouth, capable of doing the work of eight of the old pendulum saws. A circular saw, planing machines, lathes and steam masons were added, all being driven by a Robey high pressure steam engine.

In the quarries the large hand operated cranes were gradually modified to operate by steam, and, following the sale of Messrs Hill's plant at the completion of their contracts, some of the rail-mounted travelling cranes were acquired by the stone companies. A combination of old and new carried on in the industry until the introduction of electricity via the National Grid in 1930, after which some of the quarry cranes were converted to electric operation, as were many machines in the mills.

In the days before modern plant was available on construction sites a small line was often laid for a steam crane, excavator, or just for wagons to move materials about. One such 2 ft gauge line was used during the construction of the Naval oil tanks, together with the Royal Naval Officers' club and sports ground, before World War I.

At Wyke Regis, Whitehead's torpedo factory had a 2 ft gauge line running from within the factory out under the Portland branch to the end of a pier. The train was hauled by battery electric locomotives conveying torpedoes and other stores required to be shipped to the torpedo range on the breakwater. However this insignificant little railway also carried Royalty on Friday 4th April, 1902, when His Majesty King Edward VII, visiting Portland on the Royal Yacht *Victoria & Albert*, landed at the pier from the Royal Barge and travelled on the train to visit the Whitehead's factory.

At the bridge by which the tramway passed under the Portland branch, an electric crane was located so that goods could be transferred from standard gauge wagons standing in the siding above.

A line of the same type also existed on the northern arm of the breakwater to carry torpedoes and stores around the Bincleaves establishment of the Admiralty, and out along the breakwater to the torpedo testing range.

Many lines were of a temporary nature and are undocumented, so it is worth noting that as recently as 1985 a 2 ft gauge underground railway was laid in the Chiswell area during the construction of sewers. For much of the work the skip wagons were propelled by hand, but a battery locomotive was used for a while. These could well prove to be the last rails laid on Portland, bringing to a close its fascinating and complex railway history.

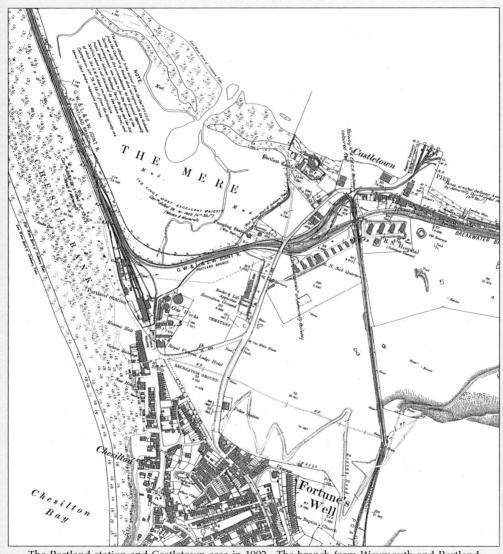

The Portland station and Castletown area in 1902. The branch from Weymouth and Portland station are to the left. The line to the dockyard (later the Easton & Church Hope Railway) curves across the map. The revised 1897 facilities at Castletown pier for the Portland Railway are clearly shown as is the incline up to the top drum.

Reproduced from the 25", 1902 Ordnance Survey Map

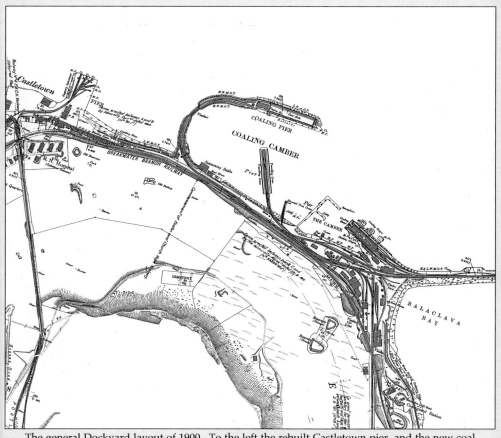

The general Dockyard layout of 1900. To the left the rebuilt Castletown pier, and the new coal jetty of 1893. The old and new stone loading jetties are shown in the centre (*illustrated on page 93*). To the right the original Dockyard works and coal stores (Monkey Island), and the Admiralty incline passing under the Easton & Church Hope Railway which skirts the Dockyard formation. *Reproduced from the 25″, 1902 Ordnance Survey Map*

The top north-west side of Portland in 1900, the Portland Railway curving around the north-west side of the Verne on the right-hand side, before crossing the map to Priory Corner. Various branches can be seen going to quarries on the left, although many earlier lines have already been lifted, note the lines crossing under Wide Street. The complex of lines around the Sawmill area of Easton Lane are shown with the Admiralty Quarry lines coming in from the right lower corner. *Reproduced from the 25", 1902 Ordnance Survey Map*

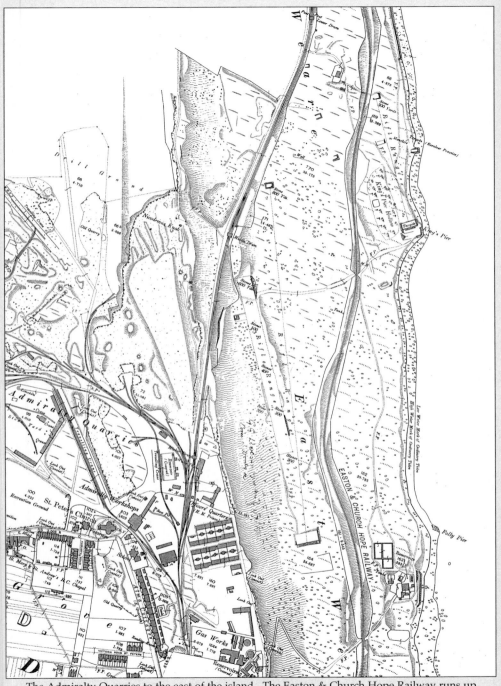

The Admiralty Quarries to the east of the island. The Easton & Church Hope Railway runs up the right-hand side. The prison is just off the bottom of the map, the Admiralty incline with the higher, middle, and lower drums clearly shown.

Reproduced from the 25", 1902 Ordnance Survey Map

Easton as in 1900, the new station and works of the Easton & Church Hope Railway dominating the centre of the map. Leading away from the centre at Sheepcroft Yard can be seen the tramway which ran from the Sawmill in Easton Lane to West Cliff. The lines from Long Acre Quarry ran across Grove Road to join the Admiralty system, Long Acre being worked by Messrs Hills for the breakwater extension.

Reproduced from the 25", 1902 Ordnance Survey Map

The top east side of the island in 1900 showing the Admiralty Quarry layout in full detail. The Portland Railway carries across the map at the top, the junctions and bridges illustrated on pages 30-32 are clearly shown, running to Waycroft, King Barrow, and Withies Croft quarries. Although it may appear so, there was no physical connection between the Portland and Admiralty systems owing to the difference of gauge!

Reproduced from the 25", 1902 Ordnance Survey Map

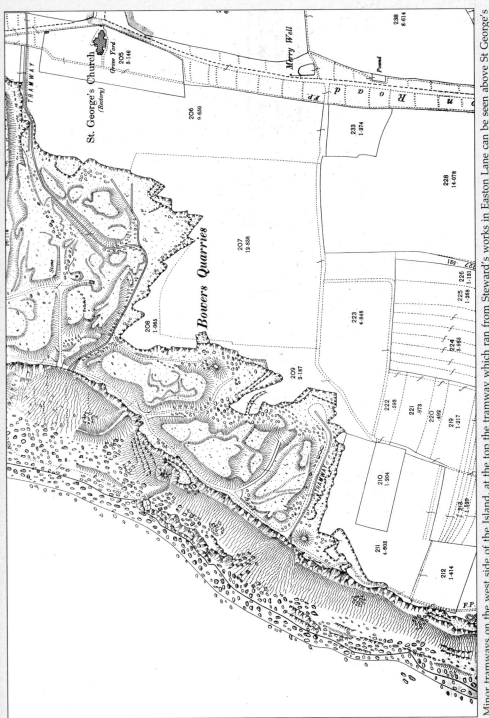

Minor tramways on the west side of the Island, at the top the tramway which ran from Steward's works in Easton Lane can be seen above St George's Church running out to the tip on the cliff face. Below can be seen another tramway running out onto the cliff face. Although not clearly shown on this or

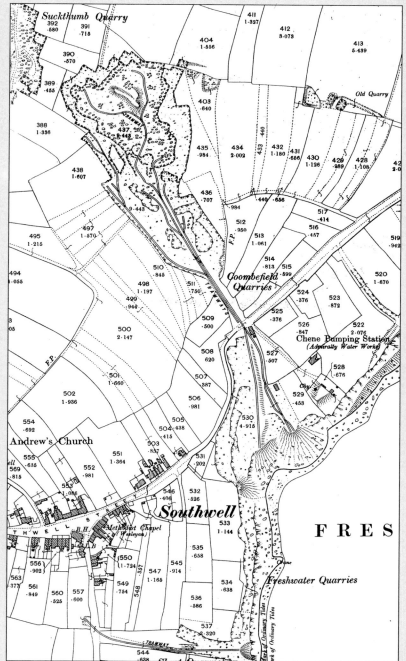

Map showing the tramways at Coombefield Quarry, north-east of Southwell. The tramway crossed the Wakeham-Southwell Road at the Old Blacksmith's shop to the cliff top tipping site. At the bottom of the map below Southwell, a short tramway crossing the Portland Bill road can be seen.

Reproduced from the 25", 1902 Ordnance Survey Map

1902 map showing the tramway at Portland Bill, by that date it was shown as disused. The only buildings in the area at the time were the Coastguard cottages, the new lighthouse, situated at the bottom end of the tramway, was not constructed until 1905. The road to the Bill, the café's and tourist interest were to come in later years.

*Reproduced from the 25",
1902 Ordnance Survey Map*

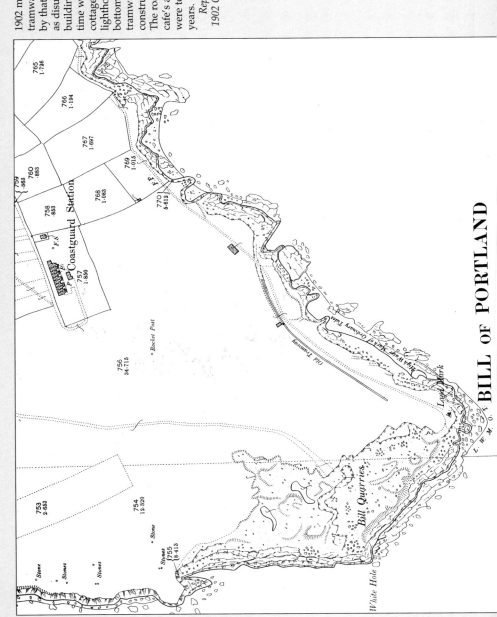

BILL OF PORTLAND

Other Known Locomotives

Perry, Cutbill & de Lungo Limited

Type	Builder/Works No.	Built	Cylinders	Wheel dia.	Weight	Note
0-6-0 ST	MW 616	1876	12 in. x 17 in.	3 ft 1⅜ in.	18 t	1

1. New to T.J. Waller Manchester, to J.D. Nowell of Todmorden. To Perry, Cutbill, & De Lungo. February 1894 Sold to Wotton Tramway (Brill branch). 1901 to Phillips Newport (Mon).

H.M. Keone Limited

Type	Builder/Works No.	Built	Cylinders	Wheel dia.	Weight	Note
0-6-0 ST	MW 1211	1891	12 in. x 18 in.	3 ft		1
0-4-0 ST	MW					2

1. New to Ecklersley, Godfrey & Liddelow, Liverpool. To Pethick Bros contractors. To H.M. Keone 1898. 1901 to Herbert Weldon, to Pauling & Company. To J.F. Wake dealer Darlington. 1916 to J.J. Charlesworth, Leeds. Scrapped by Hunslet 1932.
2. Only details known from auction details.

F. J. Barnes Limited

Type	Builder/Works No.	Built	Cylinders	Wheel dia.	Weight	Note
0-4-2 WT	BAG 970	1888	5 in. x 7½ in.	1 ft 3¼ in.		1

1. 2 ft gauge, named *Excelsior*. New to C.J. Naylor. 1895 to J. Nuttall contractor. 1898 to F. J. Barnes. Broken up locally.

Recent erosion of the cliff near Portland Bill has revealed a section of the quarry line that ran from the south of the present lighthouse, to a crane on the cliff to the east. This section of line which had been buried under infill was of the Portland Railway gauge of 4 ft 6 in.
Author

The first traction engine purchased by Messrs. F.J. Barnes, Fowler No. 6489 *Pioneer*, stands at the bottom of Fortuneswell adjacent to Albion Terrace.   *T.H. Cailes Collection*

Fowler No. 6653 *Zulu* awaits her next load in a quarry at the turn of the century. The primitive wagon and the quarry hand crane add interest to this late Victorian picture. *Author's Collection*

Chapter Five

Traction Engines of the Isle of Portland

Employed in conjunction with the 'Merchants' Railway' and other quarrying activities, the traction engine occupied an important place in the story of stone transport. Although the opening of the 'Merchants' Railway' had eliminated much of the most difficult work performed by horses, some stone was still taken down through Fortuneswell by horse-drawn carts until the turn of the century.

Jonathan Lano had introduced the first traction engine onto the island about 1875, its principal purpose being to assist with his farming activities. As Lano supplied horses to many quarry owners, there is little doubt that the engine was put through its paces hauling stone wagons at some time. However, the first involvement of the quarry owners with traction engines was not until 1891, when F.J. Barnes purchased an engine to haul stone from his quarries to his masonry works which was situated alongside the railway station in Victoria Square. Within a short period of time the advantages of steam power became apparent and further engines were purchased.

Although the majority of the Island's engines were engaged in the stone trade, a few were engaged in different work such as agriculture (already mentioned). Companies which used traction engines included Jesty & Baker of Castletown who were Government contractors, general builders, iron and brass founders and engineers. Several other people were issued with road locomotive licences, George Mitchell holding one in 1901-1902, but no details have survived. In 1904 Mitchell, who had a successful stone business in Chiswell (later known as Baker's Ground), sold out to Mr Baker of Jesty & Baker.

Likewise S.B. Jones had road locomotive licences issued in 1898, but again no details survive. E.A. Collins purchased No. 1375 (of 1888) of unidentified make, in October 1897. According to local trade directories of the period, Collins was a coal merchant and cab proprietor.

It is reputed that the Royal Navy operated traction engines in the Dockyard in the early days, and a Royal Navy steam roller was employed for a time during 1934 at HMS Osprey, Aveling & Porter No. 8876, a ten-ton T type supplied new in February 1918 to the Admiralty Air Service Construction Corp. based at Sunbury on Thames as fleet No. 1. It is believed she was with the Air Ministry at Kidbrooke in 1921, when she was registered in Surrey as PC 9024.

There were also occasions when quarry engines were employed in other work, a good example being when heavy guns had to be hauled to The Verne, East Weare, and West Weare Batteries. On 15th September, 1892 the first of three 18 ton guns for East Weare Battery was hauled to the site by Messrs Barnes Fowler No. 6489 *Pioneer*, the total weight including the carriage being about 23 tons. The *Southern Times* reported that 'the engine acted splendidly'.

In February 1909, when new 22 ton, 9.2 guns had to be delivered to Blacknor Fort, a Fowler engine of Messrs Barnes undertook the journey from the Dockyard - although to avoid any problems the guns were winched up Meissner's Knap using the wire and winch fitted to the engine.

Fowler No 10143, FX 6659 *Quartus,* climbs Fortuneswell with empty trailers returning from the Victoria Square sawmills. The property on the left was demolished in the years following World War II.   *Author's Collection*

Fowler No, 15657, FX 6661 *Kitchener,* stands at the top of Meissner's Knap in Fortuneswell before descending the slope. Note the state of both the engine and the road surface. A survivor through preservation this engine was the star of the film *The Iron Maiden* in 1962.

Author's Collection

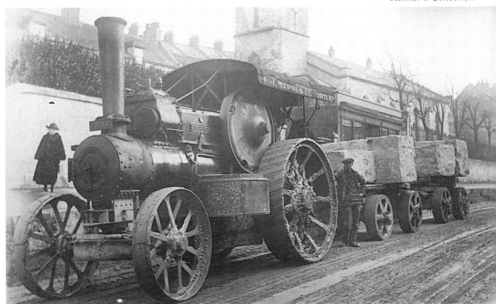

Early in 1915 Portland Council ordered a 5 ton tractor and three trailers from Burrell at a cost of £663. No doubt due to war commitments the order was delayed, and at the October Council meeting the Surveyor stated the engine was ready but there was a delay with the trailers, delivery eventually being made in November. The main use for the engine and trailers was to collect Channel Island granite that was shipped into Castletown for road maintenance, but the engine was also used to tow a trailer which acted as a dustcart!

Over the years the Council owned three rollers, all being sold in August 1932, after which date it would appear that contractors were employed on road rolling. A difficulty experienced on the island, was the rolling of roads on steep gradients, this being achieved by employing a traction engine at the top end, using its winch and wire rope to assist the roller on the ascent.

The first roller of 1890 came into prominence early in 1892 when the driver, Tom Thorne, resigned after members of the Local Board interfered whilst he was working. In July 1911 the Council decided to purchase a second roller, the tender of Messrs Aveling & Porter to supply a 12 ton machine for £543 16s. 7d. being accepted.

A late arrival on the scene was Messrs Smith & Lander who commenced trading in masonry after the Great War. They later moved to a site in Easton Lane (now Easton Masonry) in 1923, having contracts to supply headstones to the War Graves Commission and branching out into building work in later years both at Portland and Weymouth. Their first steam lorry was acquired in 1926 and was painted in a chocolate livery with white lettering. Their third wagon acquired in December 1928 was a celebrity in its own right! The Foden record sheet for No 11500 states, 'Show finish for exhibition at the British Empire Exhibition London'. It was also the first wagon fitted with the new pattern slide bars and new pattern stay rods. The firm had six vehicles by 1930 which were not only used for local work, as driver Harry Gardiner is recorded as taking loads of headstones to Dover with one of the Fodens! However the company quickly changed over to motor vehicles, exchanging several of the steam lorries with Foden. The last steam vehicle purchased from Foden by Smith & Lander was one of the infamous 'O' type, usually known as the 'Speed 6'. Designed with the best features of both steam and the motor vehicle with a specification road speed of 45 mph, it was clearly ahead of any other steam vehicle in production. However plagued with problems with the somewhat revolutionary boiler and arriving at a time when Foden was turning production over to diesel vehicles, the 'O' type was soon discontinued.

The Smith & Lander vehicle was even more of a novelty, No. 13660, completed in August 1930, was first employed by Foden as a demonstrator before purchase by Smith & Lander. It later passed to British Tar Spraying Ltd of Leeds.

The passage of time has obscured the details of some early engines, and little is known of engines employed by the J. Pearce Stone Company. On 16th May, 1892 he purchased an 8 hp Wallis & Stevens non-compound engine No. 2173 which was sold in 1898. In December 1897 a two-speed Burrell single crank compound - No. 2060 - was acquired. By 1916 it had passed to an unknown buyer. Likewise some of the early Lano and Barnes engines are not fully documented.

The fatal accident of Monday 25th July, 1921. Messrs. F.J. Barnes' Fowler No 8839 FX 6660, *Sphinx* embedded in the wall at the junction of Verne Common Road after running away down Fortuneswell. The steersman later died of his injuries. Behind stands Albion Terrace, the scene having changed very little to the present day.   *K. Lynham Collection*

Messrs F.J. Barnes' Fowler *Sphinx* yet again in trouble on Friday 8th May, 1925, when the right hand rear wheel collapsed in Fortuneswell. A second engine prepares to drag the damaged wheel clear. As can clearly be seen, it was a miracle nobody was trapped under the falling wheel!   *Author's Collection*

Lano was listed in the 1911 directory as a farmer and haulage contractor. Between 1897 and 1913 he owned at least nine different engines of various types, mostly engaged in haulage work for various quarry owners. Fowler road locomotive No. 8466 purchased in November 1899 was requisitioned by the War Department and, following overhaul by Messrs Fowler in March 1900, was sent to the Boer War. Later she was sold with other engines to the Civil Administration of South Africa.

Burrell No. 2562, purchased new in 1903, was a little light for the work required of her, and in 1909 she was sold to Richard Townsend, the Weymouth amusement caterer, to haul his 'three abreast gallopers'. Rebuilt to showman's specification, she was named *Empress of the South*. When the ride was sold in 1916 the engine passed to W. Nichols of Forest Gate, Essex, for employment in war work on Salisbury plain. By 1923 she was working a set of Chair-o-planes. Sold again in 1939 she ended her days threshing in Essex.

Another Portland engine of particular interest was Fowler No. 13092 - an 'R3' type compound road locomotive, supplied new in March 1914 to the Wilfley Mining Company of Gartham Sands. She was fitted with 'Bottrail Patent Wheels' (a series of flat plates around the wheel which allowed the engine to literally walk across soft ground). These wheels were removed the following year, and in March 1917 the engine passed to Messrs Barnes and named *Lord Kitchener*. Following the Great War she was sold to Sligo County Council.

Several other engines employed are worthy of note. The smaller engines, in particular the Garretts, were used by the riggers involved in the maintenance and moving of the fixed cranes in the quarries. The acquisition of the two Portland Council steam rollers in 1932 was understandable, as with the use of steam and motor lorries the internal roads in the quarries needed to be kept in a reasonable condition.

However the reason for the purchase of a Fowler ploughing engine in the 1930s has never been fully explained. No. 13473 was one of a pair supplied new in June 1913 to L.F. Briggs of Stamford, Lincs. When the pair was split up she moved to Portland. Something of a mystery, she is reported as having survived until cut up in 1953.

Working the engines on Portland was difficult and required great skill. The wage of a driver in 1909 was £2 a week, this being revealed at the local court when a driver was prosecuted for the theft of 28 lb. of steam coal, valued at 4½d., which he was taking home to heat a damp cottage.

Being in charge of over-loaded wagons also attracted the attention of the police. On 17th March, 1910 an engine belonging to Messrs Bagg & Sons of Weymouth hauling two trailers loaded with bricks was stopped near Victoria Square. The driver was unable to quote the number of bricks on the trailers which resulted in the load being taken to the prison (later the Borstal) where it was taken off and counted. The large wagon held 3,832 bricks whilst the smaller one held 2,686. Taking the average weight of the bricks as 7 lb. each, the large wagon held 11 ton 19 cwt. 2 qr, and the other 8 ton 7 cwt. 3 qr 14 lb., and the magistrates ordered the company to pay the costs of 7s. 6d.

The driver had already been stopped on the journey at Wyke Regis for driving a locomotive at a greater speed than 2 mph, PC Swain having estimated the load behind the engine at about 30 tons. The driver was fined 2s. 6d. with 7s. 6d. costs.

A Fowler engine of Messrs F.J. Barnes assists the Portland UDC Aveling & Porter roller whilst laying Brymers Avenue. Owning to the steep slope the winch wire of the Fowler is used to assist the roller so as not to cause slipping and damage the road surface.   *Author's Collection*

One of Messrs. F.J. Barnes' Fowler locomotives at the top of Meissner's Knap in February 1909 whilst employed in hauling new 22 ton 9.2 guns to West Weare. The engine winch cable has been let out to haul the load up the steepest part of the climb.   *T. H. Cailes Collection*

However, this case appeared to be an exception to the rule, as very few cases concerning traction engines ever appeared before the Island magistrates. To quote an old Portlander, 'The gaffers of the stone industry were also the gaffers of the local authority' hence little was ever said about the damage to the roads caused by the engines.

The stone trucks when empty weighed up to seven tons and were solidly constructed of timber with steel reinforcement. They had wooden wheels with iron-shod rims until later years, when cast-iron wheels were fitted. The only brake was a 'drug shoe' on a chain which was placed under a rear wheel when descending a hill. The engines were only a little better, having only a screw-down brake working wooden brake blocks on the rear wheels, plus the skill of the driver who could reverse his engine using steam pressure to act as a brake. With up to 50 tons, descending Portland was not a job for the apprehensive! Many drivers kept to the right-hand side (if possible) when rounding Priory Corner so that in the event of trouble the engine could be quickly turned into the bank. The appalling condition of the roads of the period, which in Winter were a sea of white mud looking like porridge, or fine dust in Summer, did little to assist the traction engine driver.

In the working environment of the late Victorian era and the early years of the present century, it is surprising that there were not a great many accidents involving traction engines as they negotiated the difficult roads of the Island.

There had been, over the years, accidents involving the men who worked them, unfortunately some fatal. In September 1892 James Pavey, a brakesman employed by Messrs Barnes, caught his sleeve in the brake wheel, resulting in serious injury. Alfred Coomb was killed in January 1900 whilst assisting with an engine and two trailers, being crushed by the wheels of one of the trailers. On 2nd August, 1918 William Wollage was struck by the tow bar whilst attempting to couple a trailer to an engine in the Council yard, and later died of his injuries, and there was also the tragic case of the driver who ran over his own son.

A run-away with a road locomotive was a recipe for total destruction, but fortunately there were few serious accidents although there are tales of many near ones! One of the first 'lucky escapes' took place on Tuesday 4th April, 1893 when an engine belonging to Messrs Barnes, believed to be Fowler No. 6489 *Pioneer*, went out of control whilst descending Fortuneswell with two loaded wagons. A report in the *Southern Times* stated:

The wheels skidded away, it is stated owing to the road having been watered. Both engine and wagons started off at a good pace owing to the heavy weight, and when near Mr Osborne's shop the driver thought it advisable to divert the engine's course. Fortunately in this he succeeded and directed the engine in a direction between Mr Osbourne and Dr Ashton's house, but in doing so the connecting rod of the engine gave way in the strain, with the result that the engine and wagons dashed ahead and collided with Mr T. Comben's house, entirely destroying the coping of the wall, while a stone from the top of the load was thrown off against one of the bay windows smashing it to fragments.

Later in the day when the engine had been repaired and continued on its

One of Messrs F.J. Barnes' Fowler locomotives at the top of Fortuneswell during the movement of 22 ton 9.2 guns to West Weare in February 1909. The engine is seen uncoupled from the load, as over the steepest parts of the climb the engine winch wire was used to haul the gun, the engine then moving forward to take another pull. *Author's Collection*

An unidentified Fowler engine hauls a load up Easton Lane, past the Drill Hall. Note the trailer with wooden wheels and iron shod rims, they have almost a 'Fred Flintstone' look about them, but were used on stone wagons for many years. *S. Morris Collection*

journey it frightened a grocer's delivery horse causing it to bolt, turning over the wagon and scattering the contents!

On 15th October, 1915, another runaway took place, the *Southern Times* describing the event thus:

> One of Messrs F.J. Barnes large traction engines with two loads of stone behind it took charge at the foot of Royal and tore down through the narrow street at an almost incredible speed, clattering and banging its way along, bringing people to their windows and doors in the fear that a daylight raid had commenced. The cause, it is stated, that the council's workmen being engaged in repairing the road at the junction of Old Hill, New Road and Verne Hill, a request was made to the traction engine drivers to cease using their big drug shoes until the road had been firmly rolled in. The engine driven by a man named Read who had taken the place of the regular driver, Smith for the day, obeyed the instruction to drive without the shoe, but, owing to the extremely greasy nature of the road surface, the engine took charge after rounding the bend and carried on all the way down Fortuneswell.
>
> The steersman stayed at the wheel some time, but Read thinking it better to have one killed than two - ordered him to jump for it, and finding him reluctant, it is said, gave him a helping hand and then took charge of the engine himself. The clutch failed to work, but the gallant driver stuck to his post, trying to let off the steam and steering so well that he passed the narrowest part of the road in safety, hoping to be able to regain control on the level between the Well and the top of Mallams. Unfortunately the way on the engine carried him past this spot, and when opposite St John's Church he was faced with the alternative of driving into the kerb or plunging down Meissner's Knap into the houses below and certain death to himself.
>
> Happily it was Saturday morning and there were no children about, and the driver chose the former alternative and steered the engine into the kerb just above Mr Norris's shop in Cheapside. The wheels struck and mounted the kerb, carrying away the low wall and rails in front of Mr Benjamin Bollen's house and then striking a similar wall of Mr W. H. Morris's private residence, throwing one of the large coping stones into the bay window of the house. Just as it struck here the two front wheels of the engine snapped off at the axles, and the engine stopped.

Although both of the above reports are seen through the eyes of a newspaper reporter and lack technical comprehension of the events, they certainly convey vividly the picture of an engine running amok in a steep narrow street.

With this method of working it was inevitable that eventually a disaster would occur, but luck held out until the morning of Monday 25th July, 1921 when *Sphinx*, a Fowler owned by F. J. Barnes & Company, ran out of control down Meissner's Knapp in Fortuneswell with two fully loaded wagons. Eye witness accounts told of how the engine quickly gathered speed, and that in an effort to control it the crew turned the engine towards Verne Common Road hoping to stop on the uphill grade. Unfortunately a motor vehicle blocked their path, resulting in the engine coming to an abrupt halt after smashing through a solid stone wall at the junction, the front trailer loaded with 14 blocks of stone running over the back of the engine and crushing the steersman, George White, who later died of his injuries.

At the inquest Robert White, brother of the driver and cousin of the steersman, said that he was the look-out man walking behind the trucks. They had about 6½ tons of stone on each truck, which was an ordinary load. He first noticed something was wrong near Digby's shop. All of a sudden the engine

Engines stand at Priory Corner with stone waiting to be transferred to the Portland Railway. In the foreground are two Fowler locomotives, and behind them a Burrell. Note the state of the road by the leading engine!   *Author's Collection*

F.J. Barnes' Fowler No 15319, FX 7850 *Nellie* descending New Road (between Priory Corner and Fortuneswell) with two loaded trailers. Note the primitive construction of these vehicles, the lack of securing chains for the load, and the lookout man hanging on the rear. Apart from the engine, the only other form of brake is the 'drug shoe' to be seen under the rear offside wheel of the second trailer.   *E. Latcham Collection*

and trucks were gone and all he saw was a cloud of dust. Before that they were going very slowly, as a little further back he had put two drag shoes under the wheels of the wagons. The driver, also named George White, practically knew nothing about it, 'they were only doing their very best', and did not know what caused the accident. 'Something went wrong', he said.

Edward Comben, the local baker, said 'the engine passed his shop at a fairly good pace, and a load of stone fell off at the corner owing to the back truck swaying'. Another witness stated 'the engine was going down the hill at between 40 and 50 mph'! When the engine was examined it was discovered that the pin that should have been inserted in the gear change lever to hold it in the selected position was not in place, it later being found in the coal bunker.

A verdict of accidental death was recorded. It was clear that the engine had come out of gear and run away completely out of control, gaining speed as it went, the rear wagon swaying from side to side with large blocks of stone being shaken off. With a street full of pedestrians who scattered in all directions, it was a miracle that nobody was injured. The engine crew who could have jumped clear saved what could have well been a major disaster. It did, however, emphasise the danger on such a steep hill, although it was to be another 10 years before the traction engine was replaced.

Almost five years later *Sphinx* was again in trouble when, in May 1925, as she was proceeding up Fortuneswell by the Royal Hotel, the right-hand rear wheel fell off, the spokes all breaking away at the hub. It was fortunate that passing pedestrians were not crushed by the falling wheel.

By the mid-1920s the road locomotive was losing favour as the motor lorry developed, and its decline was hastened by the implementation of the Salter Report of 1926, which resulted in the owners of steam vehicles having to pay higher taxes for a given size of vehicle with a lower legal pay load than was permitted for petrol and diesel lorries of the same size. Under the 1927 taxation rules a 12 ton road locomotive had its road tax doubled from £30 to £60 per year! There was also the forthcoming problem of the prohibition of untyred wheels on the public highway.

At the passing of the 1930 Road Traffic Act Messrs. Barnes had four road locomotives in service whilst Bath & Portland had seven, two of which were only four years old, and another only just delivered. One feels obliged to ask why such a late investment was made in what was clearly fast becoming an obsolete form of transport, the answer being that the motor lorry - although developing rapidly - was not yet suited for the work required on Portland. At the time two Sentinel DG6 three-way tipping steam wagons, owned by Newman & Masters of Lytchett Minster, were engaged in hauling rubble stone from Portland for the construction of the new Westwey Road in Weymouth. No doubt the Directors of Barnes were impressed with what they saw and in 1931 ordered two such vehicles, each costing about £1,200. The following year a second pair was ordered, and Bath & Portland ordered four of the same type. Barnes went to the extent of constructing a new building to house the vehicles at their Victoria Square yard.

The *Dorset Daily Echo* of 28th June, 1933 remarked:

Fowler No 15319, FX 7850 *Nellie* enters Victoria Square with two trailers loaded with stone destined for Messrs F.J. Barnes' mills alongside the station yard. *Author's Collection*

Fowler No. 15319, FX 7850, in her rebuilt form as a showman's locomotive and renamed *Queen Mary*. Displayed at Chipperfield's fair Weymouth, during her early days in preservation. *Author's Collection*

In spite of all the drought our main roads remain dustless thanks to the abolition of the traction engines and the substitution of the eight steam lorries which do all the work today.   Yesterday on the steam lorries 'Birthday' there were presents for the elder brethren - brand new rubber tyres, forced on at the Easton foundry.

This was one of the problems with the new vehicles: solid rubber tyres quickly wore out, and more so under quarry conditions, and were expensive to replace and difficult to fit. The solid-tyred steam lorry was restricted to 16 mph, whereas the motor vehicle could travel at 30 mph, and it also had to stop when the fire needed attention unless two men were employed. This made them unsuitable for all but very local work. The amalgamation of the two companies in 1934 created a combined fleet, although the Barnes livery was retained for a few years. The *Southern Times* for 6th January, 1934, commenting on the merger, stated: 'The combination has permitted the taking off the roads of two of the steam lorries employed in the conveyance of stone. Four more men are thereby thrown out of work. There is also, of course, the savings of the fees for road licences of the two lorries.' The remaining Sentinels continued to convey stone around the Island, although by law their gross weight could not exceed 19 tons. They were without a doubt less of a problem on the roads than their predecessors.

Meanwhile the development of the heavy lorry had progressed rapidly during the early 1930s. In September 1936 Bath & Portland purchased their first two heavy lorries - a pair of AEC Monarch tippers, and in the following January the first AEC Mamoth Major eight-wheeler joined the fleet. One steam lorry, TK 8008, had already been withdrawn at the end of 1935, to be followed by TK 8007 at the end of 1938. The remainder were withdrawn in 1939, and all were broken up on the Island except TK 7083 which passed to Southampton Corporation and survived until 1941.

Returning to the traction engines, it was with the annual Portland Fair that the road locomotive first became a familiar sight. A locomotive owned by William Handcock of Bristol hauled his switchback railway to the fair in November 1892, and several years previously sets of steam roundabouts were noted at the fair, but history has not recorded the first appearance of a traction engine at the event.

It is therefore interesting that, following the 1930 Act, nine of the former Portland engines were disposed of to showmen and saw their final working years out with travelling fairs. Showmen still required that type of engine for hauling their trains of equipment and generating power at the fairground. A showman's locomotive was simply a contractor's-type haulage engine fitted with a dynamo on an extension forward of the smokebox, a full length canopy, and the brass embellishments so beloved of showmen, and during those depression years a good second-hand engine rebuilt was less expensive than a new one built to order.

Owing to this policy, two of Barnes' Fowlers survive to the present day. No. 15319, FX 7850, was purchased by Townsend & Sons of Weymouth and following conversion by Eddison of Dorchester who fitted her with a Burrell-type showman's canopy she was put to work with 'Speedway Ark', a duty she continued until the late 1940s making appearances at the annual Portland Fair

An early view, thought to be of Wallis & Stevens' engine No. 2173, owned by John Pearce, quarry owner.   *S. Morris Collection*

An unidentified Burrell road locomotive stands at Priory Corner as stone is transferred onto the Portland Railway. Everybody poses for the camera, a typical scene from Portland's industrial past. Note the hand operated crane, the interesting point blade, and the spare wagon wheels just lying about cluttering up the working space!   *S. Morris Collection*

each November. No. 15657, FX 6661 *Kitchener*, was purchased by Mrs Oadby, rebuilt to showman's specification by Fowler's, and travelled the Midlands until purchased by H. Hollingsworth of Conisburgh in 1952. In preservation 10 years later she starred in the film *The Iron Maiden*, since when she has carried two different nameplates - *Kitchener* on one side, *The Iron Maiden* on the other! Later she was sold to Cornish owners.

No. 14863, FX 6689, passed to Jennings Bros of Devizes, and following conversion was named *Excelsior*. In 1938 she passed to H. Symonds of Brixton, London, and was renamed *Shamrock*. Sister engine No. 14864, FX 6682, also passed to Jennings Bros and was named *Edgar*.

The Burrells in the Bath & Portland fleet were also quickly acquired by showmen, Charles Heal & Sons of Glastonbury purchased two, No. 3980, PR 2474, was the first of the post-war contractor's type to be converted to showman's use, and was named *Her Majesty*. She was resold in 1941 to A. Lock of Taunton to work his 'Noah's Ark', but the following year the engine and ride passed to Armstrong of Long Eaton, Nottingham. No. 4038, PR 6162, was named *England's Glory* and stayed with Heal's until late 1946.

No. 4042, PR 7233, passed to Ernest Robinson of Barnsley. Named *Robin Hood*, she remained in use until late 1946. No. 4091, TK 4916 *Royal Manor*, went to Scotland working for Cododa, the well-known Glasgow showland family. Although fitted with a dynamo support and full length canopy and the then legal requirement of rubber tyres, she carried no adornments whatsoever. It is recorded that she was painted dark brown, with dark red wheels fully lined, but with the difficulties of war she last appeared on the road during 1943.

Last to leave the Island in August 1935 was No. 3648, FX 6685 *Jellicoe*, which was sold to George Baker of Southampton, who was both a showman and haulage contractor. Converted to a 'showman's' she had a nomadic existence, passing to Fred Gray of Kensal Green, London, then to Wall Bros of Petersfield, then returning to London under the ownership of Harry Gray of Battersea. Last licensed for showman's use in June 1939, she was still standing in Hardwick's scrap yard at West Ewell during 1947.

Seven various locomotives and rollers are now in preservation, having been initially saved by Mr E.D.K. Coombe of Portland. His first purchase was a local engine, Fowler No. 15319, FX 7850 *Queen Mary*, from Townsend's Amusement caterers of Weymouth in 1950. Later she passed to W.M. Salmon of Weymouth and later to mid-Wales, before being acquired in June 1971 by A.D. Fowler of Bemire Green. Two years later she passed to K.S.W. Cook, and today makes regular appearances at rallies in the South of England.

A second local engine, Aveling & Porter roller No. 7553 (FX 7093), from the Bath & Portland Stone Firms sadly later passed to the breakers. However Burrell showman's No. 3483, NR 9110 *Perseverance II*, purchased in 1953 passed to other enthusiasts, and today can be seen at various rallies, as can Burrell showman's No. 3938, XL 9086 *Quo Vadis*. Purchased from Hardwick's scrap yard in 1956, she was returned to operational condition before being acquired by the late Edward Hine who rebuilt her to be the finest 'showman's' seen at rallies.

Being involved in the stone industry, Coombe put one engine he had purchased to commercial use. Sentinel S4 No. 9027, CG 6473, was purchased

Three interesting close up views of Burrell road locomotives employed in the Portland stone trade. Unfortunately the passage of time has robbed us of any details of the men or engines involved.   *Author's Collection*

Bath & Portland Stone Firm's Burrell No. 3648 FX 6685 *Jellicoe* hauls a loaded trailer along Straits, into Easton Square. The motor cyclist wisely keeps well away, whilst the people opposite take no notice of what was then a daily scene!   *Author's Collection*

Bath & Portland Stone Firm's Burrell, No. 3980 PR 2474, stands in a Portland quarry. Sitting upon the engine is the driver Jack Scard. No. 2474 was built in 1924 and following sale in 1932 was converted to showman's use for Charles Heal of Glastonbury and named *Her Majesty*.
                                                                                          Author's Collection

A scene in later years, with Bath & Portland Stone Firms' Burrell No. 3648 *Jellicoe* standing at Priory Corner as stone is unloaded from the trailer to be forwarded via the Portland Railway.

P. Trim Collection

Portland UDC Burrell tractor No. 3685, FX 3326 stands in Easton Square whilst in use hauling a dust cart.

Author's Collection

Plenty of scope here for a caption contest! A sailor aboard Aveling & Porter No. 8876. Was he of Coxswain, or Stoker, rank? What we can be certain of was that the roller belonged to the Royal Navy, and was working at HMS Osprey.   *Author's Collection*

from R.M. Wooley of Bucknell, Shropshire, and put to work hauling materials for South Western Limestones. Unfortunately a fire destroyed the cab, and this final commercial venture in steam ended in the scrap yard.

In 1964 Babcock & Wilcox 10 ton roller No. 95/4014, supplied new in 1926 to Messrs W.W. Buncombe of Highbridge, was acquired by Weymouth builder Mr Foster, and was used on Portland to roll roads on a new estate. In 1966 she passed to Jack Hedges, an enthusiast who was boilersmith at Weymouth engine shed, who named her *Monarch*. Sold in 1977 she has moved on in preservation, technically having been the last 'working' engine on the Island!

The final preservation scheme on the Island commenced in 1963, when the late Peter Wallis acquired Garrett tractor No. 33305, HT 7712. New in 1918 to the War Department, she later passed through Kent owners and was converted to a showman's tractor, reverting to agricultural work during the 1939-45 war. Over several years she was returned to showman's condition at Portland, and in 1998 passed to Kent owners.

Portland Traction Engines Ownership List

Prior to the Motor Car Act of 1904, the only vehicles that had to be registered were locomotives (over 3 tons) which were registered under the Locomotive Act of 1898 and allotted numbers carried on small plates supplied by the respective County Councils.

Following the 1904 Act other mechanically propelled vehicles were treated as 'carriages' and were liable for licence duty, as were private horse-dawn carriages. Following the Roads Act of 1920, which came into force the following year, heavy locomotives were brought into line and received registration numbers. With this mass registration, the general rule that the registration number gives the age of the vehicle in relationship to others failed to apply, as can be seen from the following ownership tables. For example, FX 7094 dates from 1890 whilst FX 6661 only dates from 1920.

Owing to the lack of fully detailed records pre-1921, and the fact that the second part of the FX register never passed to the Dorset County Record Office, there have been difficulties in compiling complete ownership lists. Also with the passage of time, some early engines have failed to be recorded.

Abbreviations

AP	Aveling & Porter	RR	Road roller
B	Burrell	RL	Road locomotive
B&W	Babcock & Wilcox	SHL	Showman's road locomotive
JF	John Fowler	WGN	Steam wagon
F	Foden	PE	Ploughing engine
G	Garrett	TR	Steam tractor
ML	Marshall	LL	Last licensed
RSJ	Ransome, Sims & Jefferies	LO	Last registered owner
SS	Sentinel	**	Still in existence
W&S	Wallis & Stevens	N/SH	New (N) or acquired (A)

Messrs F.J. Barnes' first Sentinel DG6 steam wagon, No. 8619 TK 7082, stands outside the Sentinel factory at Shrewsbury before delivery. Seated in the cab is Portland driver Jess Bishop.
Author's Collection

The four Sentinel 'super six' wagons after delivery to the Bath & Portland Stone Firms Company in 1932. All four are still displaying delivery trade plates. From left to right Nos. 3, 4, 2, 1.
Author's Collection

F.J. Barnes, Easton, Portland

Make	No.	Type	Built	N/SH	Name	Reg. No.	Notes
JF	6489	TE	12/91	N	*Pioneer*	FX 6657	6
B	3648	RL	10/15	N	*Jellicoe*	FX 6685	12
JF	6492	TE	3/92	A 11/92	*Pioneer*		10
JF	4472	TE	3/83	A 7/93			LL 4/13
JF	6653	RL	3/93	A 11/96	*Zulu*		LL 4/13, 5
JF	8466	RL	11/99	N	*Sphinx*	WD 1900	12
JF	8839	RL	5/00	N	*Sphinx*	FX 6660	LO F.J. Barnes. 7
JF	9985	RL	6/04	N	*Quartus*	FX 6659	LO F.J. Barnes
JF	10143	RL	6/05	N	*Quintus*		
JF	13092	RL	3/14	A	*Lord Kitchener*		13
JF	14863	RL	3/17	A		FX 6689	11
JF	14864	RL	3/17	N		FX 6682	14
JF	15657	RL	9/20	N	*Kitchener*	FX 6661	** 8
JF	15319	RL	1/19	A	*Nellie*	FX 7850	** 2
JF		RL		A /26		HT 3077	
JF	10301	RL	3/08	A /25		HR 3346	3
	805	RL		A /02			LL 10/04
G	30929	TE	6/12	A 9/17		BJ 1369	4
SS	8619	WGN	12/31	N		TK 7082	1
SS	8620	WGN	12/31	N		TK 7083	1
SS	8716	WGN	6/32	N		TK 8007	1
SS	8717	WGN	6/32	N		TK 8008	1
AP	7553	RR	12/11	A 8/32		FX 7093	9, 1

Notes

1. To Bath & Portland Stone Company upon take over.
2. New to WD , 1921 to F.J. Barnes, to Richard Townsend & Sons Weymouth converted to showman's locomotive, named *Queen Mary*. 1950 to E.D.K. Coombe Portland, to W.M. Salmon, 1971 to A.D. Fowler Bemire Green. 1973 to K.W.S. Cook.
3. Ex-R. Hodder.
4. Ex-Yeovil area owner.
5. Ex-T. Francis.
6. LO F.J. Barnes. LL 31/12/24.
7. Involved in fatal runaway Fortuneswell July 1921.
8. 1932 to Mrs H. Oadley & Sons Alfreton Derbyshire, converted to showman's. 1952 to H. Hollingsworth Conisburgh. 1955 to S.J. Crawley, Turvey, Beds. 1965 to W.G. Hawkins, St Issey, Cornwall. 1991 A. Marchington,Buxsworth, Derbyshire.
9. 12 ton road roller ex-Portland UDC 8/32
10. Ex-Leeds Co-op.
11. Ex-Ministry of Munitions, to F.J. Barnes by 1921, to Jennings of Devizes 3/33, converted to showman's locomotive named *Excelsior*. 1938 to H. Symonds, London renamed *Shamrock* LL 30/6/44.
12. Requisitioned by WD 1/00, overhauled by Fowler, 3/00 to South Africa, Boer War.
13. New 3/14 to Wilfley Mining Company Gartham Sands, 17/3/17 to F.J. Barnes. 1920 to Sligo County Council.
14. To Jennings Bros, Devizes 3/33.

The last to leave the island was Burrell No. 3648 *Jellicoe* sold to haulier and amusement caterer George Baker of Southampton; the final journey photographed at Priory Corner in August 1935. Towed by a Foden overtype, one of the Bath & Portland Sentinels acts as an extra brake descending the steep hill.

K. Lynham Collection

J. Lano & Sons

Make	No.	Type	Built	N/SH	Name	Reg. No.	Notes
JF	6492	TE	3/92	A /97		LL 1903	2
B	2083	RL	5/98	N			1, 5
B	243	RL	11/01	N			1
B	2549	RL	1/03	N	Britannia		1
B	2562	RL	4/03	N			4
AP	5443	RL	3/04	N			1
AP	5634	RL	11/04	N			6
RS	14635	TE	10/02	A			3

1. To Bath & Portland Stone Company 1913.
2. Purchased from F.J. Barnes 1897.
3. From C. Bowley, Slindon, to Lott & Walne, Dorchester in 1908. To Lano c. 1915. Registered with Dorset County Council 8/15 as agricultural engine.
4. Sold 1909 to Richard Townsend & Sons Weymouth, converted to showman's, named *Empress of the South*. Sold 1916 W. Nichols, Essex. Out of showman's use 1939. Last used Threshing in Essex. 1921 registered as HR 3896.
5. Dorset County Council No. 299.
6. Sold 1908 to Hawkley Bros. Dudbridge.

Bath & Portland Stone Firms

Make	No.	Type	Built	N/SH	Name	Reg. No.	Notes
B	2083	RL	5/98	A /13			1, 15
B	2436	RL	11/01	A /13			1, 16
B	2549	RL	1/03	A /13	Britannia	FX 6684	LL 24/3/32. LO B&P 1
AP	5443	RL	3/04	A /13			17, 1
B	1938	TE	7/96	A 10/14		FX 6686	2, 13
JF	14882	TE	4/17	A		FX 6688	LO B&P
B	3980	RL	4/24	N		PR 2474	9
B	4038	RL	1/26	N		PR 6162	5
B	4042	RL	6/26	N		PR 7233	6
B	4091	RL	6/30	N	Royal Manor	TK 4916	7
W&S	7397		7/13	N		AA 1599	
G	31193		5/13	A		BJ 1659	**, 8
G	33288		5/18	A 8/23		PR 1314	3
SS	8685	WGN	3/32	N		TK 7548	LL 7/39 LO B&P
SS	8686	WGN	3/32	N		TK 7549	LL 7/39 LO B&P
SS	8687	WGN	4/32	N		TK 7674	
SS	8688	WGN	4/32	N		TK 7675	LL 7/39 LO B&P
SS	8619	WGN	12/31	N		TK 7082	LO B&P, 10
SS	8620	WGN	12/31	N		TK 7083	10, 11
SS	8716	WGN	6/32	N		TK 8007	LO B&P, 10
SS	8717	WGN	6/32	N		TK 8008	LL 12/35 LO B&P, 10
AP	2619	RR	3/90	A 8/32		FX 7094	LL 31/12/40 LO B&P
AP	7553	RR	12/11	A		FX 7093	10, 4
JF	13473	PE	6/13	A		CT 4287	14

1. Ex-J. Lano 1913
2. Ex-C. Noyce.
3. Purchased ex-WD sale, later to Welshpool owner. LL 6/34
4. 15 ton road roller. To E.D.K. Coombe, LL 31/12/56. LO Pollock Brown, Southampton, breakers. Broken up 30/11/56.
5. To Charles Heal Bristol, converted to showman's LL 30/6/46. LO C. Heal.
6. To Ernest Robinson Barnsley, converted to showman's, named *Robin Hood* LL 30/9/46.LO E. Brook Sheffield, broken up 1/5/54.
7. to Mrs Codona, Glasgow, converted to showman's. LL 31/3/43.
8. To Corfield, Abermule. Later preserved by Fry in Somerset, named *Henrietta*, rebuilt as a showman's tractor, renamed *Yeovil Town*. Sold to owner in Castleford, Yorks. renamed *The Star*.
9. To Charles Heal, Bristol converted to showman's, LL 30/9/54. LO Armstrong Nottingham.
10. Ex-F.J. Barnes, upon take over of company 1934.
11. LO County Borough of Southampton. LL 5/41.
12. To G. Baker showman & Haulage contractor Southampton, to Fred Gray, Hants. To Wall Bros, Hants. To Harry Gray, Battersea, London. LL 30/6/39. Still in Hardwick's scrapyard 1947.
13. Lo Scorce Bros. Chickerell, Weymouth. Scrap dealer. Broken up 12/27.
14. New to L.F. Briggs, Stamford, Lincs. Cut up 1953.
15. To Lott & Walne, Dorchester 1917.
16. To W. Morris Cardiff.
17. To E. Cavanagh.

Foden 'D' type wagon No. 13198. TK 1702. New to Smith & Lander, this 12 ton six-wheeler is
seen having collected coal from Easton station yard in June 1929. Driver Harry Birkin leans out
of the cab, whilst mate Harry Gardner stands alongside.   *H. Gardner Collection*

A sign of the changing times, transferring an export order of stone from a Bath & Portland Stone
Firms Company AEC Mammoth Major lorry into a railway wagon under the gantry at
Castletown sidings during the late 1940s. Pre-war this stone would have been hauled from the
quarry to Priory Corner by traction engine, then travelled over the Portland Railway to
Castletown sidings. Within a few years heavy lorries would replace rail transport altogether.
                                                                    Author's Collection

Portland Urban District Council

Make	No.	Type	Built	N/SH	Name	Reg. No.	Notes
AP	2619	RR	3/90	N		FX 7094	2, 5
AP	7553	RR	12/11	N		FX 7093	3
ML	80941	RR	4/26	N		PR 6670	4
B	3685	TR	11/15	N		FX 3326	1

1. Painted in a lake livery. 8/32 sold to Cull, Chard, Somerset.
2. 15 ton roller, sold 8/32 to Bath & Portland Stone Firms.
3. 12 ton roller, sold 8/32 to F.J. Barnes.
4. Sold 8/32, LL 31/12/49. LO Pollock Brown Southampton scrap dealers. Broken up 27/3/53
5. Operated by the Local Board prior to the setting up of the UDC.

W.H. Baker & Son, Castletown

Make	No.	Type	Built	N/SH	Name	Reg. No.	Notes
F	2588	WGN	1/11	A		M 3188	1

1. Acquired from Wheeler. 1927 sold to Jesty & Baker.

Jestey & Baker, Castletown

Make	No.	Type	Built	N/SH	Name	Reg. No.	Notes
WS	2579	TR	11/01	N	Enterprise	FX 155	3
G	28079	TR	12/08	A		BJ 795	1
F	2588	WGN	1/11	A /27		M 3188	2

1. New to A Barkus. Sold to Jones Taunton.
2. Ex-W.H. Baker 1927. Scrapped 3/31
3. Not registered under the 1920 RTA (1921)

Smith & Lander

Make	No.	Type	Built	N/SH	Name	Reg. No.	Notes
F	2294	WGN	9/10	A /26		M 2798	2
F	11500	WGN	11/24	A 12/28		TP 408	1
F	13198	WGN	11/28	N		TK 1702	3
F	7708	WGN	2/18	A /30		M 9563	4
F	8498	WGN	/18	A /30		M 9875	4
F	13660	WGN	8/30	A			5

1. Acquired 12/28 Ex J. Kiln. Sold 1929 to Stoneham UDC.
2. Acquired 2nd hand from Foden, still licenced 1930. Reputed to have ended as power unit in Easton lane works.
3. Returned to Foden 12/32, exchanged for motor lorry.
4. New to Weymouth Consumers Gas Company. Sold to Smith & Lander via J. Pitman, to Foden 1932 exchanged for motor lorries.
5. O type, Speed 6. New as Foden demonstrator, to Smith & Lander, to British Tar Spraying, Leeds.

E.A. Collins

Make	No.	Type	Built	N/SH	Name	Reg. No.	Notes
1375			/88	A 10/97			

John Pearce

Make	No.	Type	Built	N/SH	Name	Reg. No.	Notes
WS	2173	TE	5/92	N			1
B	2060	GP	12/97	N			2

1. Sold 1898 to Mr J. Drury.
2. Sold by 1916 buyer unknown.

South Western Limestones

Make	No.	Type	Built	N/SH	Name	Reg. No.	Notes
SS	9027	WGN	7/34	A /55		CG 6473	1

1. S4 wagon, acquired ex-R. M. Woolley, Bucknell, Salop 1955. 1957 vehicle burnt out, driver left a coat draped over the boiler overnight!

Foster

Make	No.	Type	Built	N/SH	Name	Reg. No.	Notes
B&W	95/4014	RR	/26	A /64		YB 5088	1

1. Ex-W.W. Buncombe, Highbridge. To W.J. Hedges 1966. To A. Taylor Otterbourne, Hants, 1977. To R. Meader, Camp Moor, Hants 1980. To M. Doherty, North Stoneham, Hants. 1987. (Babcock & Wilcox absorbed Clayton & Shuttleworth in 1924.)

E.D.K. Coombe

Make	No.	Type	Built	N/SH	Name	Reg. No.	Notes
JF	15319	RL		A	Queen Mary	FX 7850	**, 1
JF	12749	RL		A		XC 9654	2
AP	7553	RR	/11	A		FX 7093	3
B	3483	HL	/13	A /53	Perseverance II	WR 9110	**, 4
SS		WGN		A /53		CML 734	
SS		WGN		A /53		CML 969	
B	3938	SHL		A /56	Quo Vadis	XL 9086	**, 5
WS	7782	RR	/22	A /56		UU 788	**, 6
SS	9027	WGN	/34	A /59		CG 6473	7
WS	8033	RR	/30	A /61		OU 5185	**, 8
AP	12400	RR	/29	A /63		TK 2922	**, 9
JF	18045	RR	/31	A		TK 6141	**, 10

1. Ex-Townsend & Sons Amusement caterers Weymouth 1950. Sold to W.M. Salmon.
2. Ex-H. Goodyear. Sold 1954 to Pollock Brown, Southampton, scrapped.
3. Ex-Bath & Portland Stone Firms. Sold 1954 Pollock Brown, Southampton, scrapped.
4. Ex-Mrs Cole Amusement caterer. Sold to L.J. Casley.
5. Ex-Hardwick & Sons, scrapyard. Sold 1963 to E. Hine.
6. Ex-Hardwick & Sons, scrapyard. Sold 1959.
7. Ex-South Western Lime stone. Later scrapped.
8. Ex-Hardwick & Sons, scrapyard. Later sold.
9. Ex-Hine & Sons, Gillingham. Sold 1971 L. Way.
10. Ex-Sharp & Sons, Blandford. Sold 1968.

[Publisher's Note: there will be an Index to this volume in Volume Two.]